Two Papers

by

JOHN LAYARD

I. "THE INCEST TABOO AND THE VIRGIN ARCHETYPE"
(1945)

II. "ON PSYCHIC CONSCIOUSNESS"
(1959)

1972

DUNQUIN SERIES 5

Spring Publications
Postfach 190
8024 Zürich
Switzerland

(Second Unrevised Printing, 1977)

ISBN 0-88214-205-4

Copyright © 1972, 1977, John Layard Heirs

Photo-offset and Manufactured in Switzerland
by Buchdruckerei Schrumpf, 8123 Ebmatingen Zürich,
for Spring Publications, Postfach 190, 8024 Zürich

ACKNOWLEDGEMENTS

The two papers re-published here appeared first in the *Eranos Jahrbücher*, Volume XII/1945 (a Festschrift in honour of the seventieth birthday of C. G. Jung) and Volume XXVIII/1959. The *Eranos Jahrbücher* were published by Rhein Verlag of Zürich to whom this present volume acknowledges its thanks for the original printing from which this edition has been copied. Page numbers of the original have been retained. Tables of Contents have been placed at the beginning of each of the papers. The bibliography of the writings of John Layard was prepared by R. John Woolger. The book was conceived in tribute to the author's eightieth birthday.

THE INCEST TABOO AND THE VIRGIN ARCHETYPE

By JOHN LAYARD

CONTENTS

	page
1. *Introduction*	254
Two-fold purpose of the taboo	254
Eve the negative *anima*-projection, called the "diseased will"	256
Divine incestuous union before the Fall	259
Basic nature of incest desire. Taboo not instituted on biological grounds, but is a sacrificial system with both manifest and latent content	260
2. *Manifest purpose* of the taboo: the "*anima* without", leading to the expansion of society	266
Systematised in-breeding among Australian tribes. "Cellular" or "closed" kinship systems	266
Marriage with the mother's brother's daughter	270
Dual Organization and the 4-section kinship-system	272
Expansion beyond the limits of the 4-section system	277
3. *Latent or inner purpose* of the taboo: – The realisation of the "*anima* within"	281
Internalisation through Sacrifice. The Psychology of Celibacy	
4. *Virginity*	288
Virginity as spiritual pregnancy	288
Virginity as the "magic circle" of individuation	295
Dreams demonstrating the inner meaning of Virginity as Pregnant Womanhood (with special reference to four ancestresses of Christ)	297

1.
INTRODUCTION

Two-fold purpose of the taboo

As a tribute to Professor Jung's life-long work on the anima and on the archetypes associated with it, I propose in this essay to put forward certain conclusions that can, I think, legitimately be drawn regarding the origin and two-fold purpose of the Incest Taboo, and on the problem of Virginity to which it gives rise. While agreeing with Freud in rejecting the popular notion that the incest taboo, had any hygienic motive such as the prevention of inbreeding on biological grounds, or indeed any theory that would pre-suppose a definitely conscious purpose, I shall nevertheless part company with him in his interpretation of the anthropological data; and shall suggest that, far from being due to an Oedipus Complex which arose at a comparatively late stage in the growth of civilisation, the taboo owes its origin to the sacrificial principle which aims, so far as human affairs are concerned, at the ultimate transformation of instinct into spirit. This is itself, however, but a second stage following on the preceeding and complementary opposite creation by the spirit, represented by the Word, of instinct called in biblical language the Flesh.

For an account of the first stage we have to rely mainly on Scripture and primitive mythology and on our own ability to interpret them. For the second, however, we have sure anthropological evidence, and it is to this that I propose to devote the major part of this paper, showing how the incest taboo has both a manifest and a latent purpose, both of which (as in dreams) are unknown to the conscious minds of those who put the taboo into practice, and particularly to the majority of ordinary folk for whom the word "taboo" and its world-wide equivalents appears often to have a purely negative meaning. For, like most laws whether written or not, the taboo says only what you may not do, and as such has simply to be obeyed, whereas it is the task of those seeking to probe into the inner meaning of things to try to find out, what is the positive purpose behind it.

What I therefore propose to do is to examine first, very briefly and with biblical assistance, the hypothetical condition before the taboo came into existence, and then to follow the course of its two divergent and complementary opposite results, which are:

a) the manifest result in terms of primitive social organisation, with special reference to the very early so-called "class" or "sectional" systems of kinship; this is the problem of the "anima without", that is to say the anima externalised in the form of a wife; and

b) the latent and ultimate result in terms of the psychological or spritual effect which kinship organisation produces in the psyche of individual men, in other words the realisation of the "anima within".

This contrast I propose here to illustrate by means of biblical analogy in terms, on the one hand, of the physically pregnant Eve representing the externalised anima in the form of the actual wife together with the projections made by the man upon her, and, on the other hand, of the spiritually pregnant Mary, the Virgin, called by the Church the Second Eve, who represents the internalised anima or positive mother-image within the psyche.

And as it is the development of this latter which I believe to be the real aim of the whole process initiated by the taboo, this will inevitably in turn lead on to a discussion of the inner meaning of "virginity", which in its spiritual sense is the ultimate goal towards which the incest taboo leads, demanding as it does the highest possible development of the transformed sexual instinct in terms of the union of the soul (considered always and in both sexes as being female) with God. This inner meaning of virginity I shall then illustrate by means of dreams dreamt by members of both sexes showing how "virginity" on the psychological or spiritual level is quite independant of the presence or absence of virginity in the flesh, and may on the one hand result in the complete inner unity or spiritual pregnancy of the priestly celibate or on the other hand in physical pregnancy in cases in which this has not previously been achieved.

Eve the negative anima projection, called the "diseased will"

If spiritual virginity thus leads to successful pregnancy, it is clear that the whole subject of the incest taboo is highly paradoxical. Thus, it is worth while noting that both Old and New Testaments begin by a complete reversal of the order of nature, though in opposite directions. Thus, in the Old Testament, when God made Eve out of Adam's rib, woman was born from man instead of man from woman. The motive is repeated in Jeremiah, 30, 6, when the Lord says: "Ask ye now, and see whether a man doth travail with child?" The question was in each case: What sort of woman did he bring forth?" Was it a positive anima-image or a negative one? Jeremiah is foreshadowing the positive one. In Adam's case, however, that which he brought forth became the temptress, for the first thing she did was to deceive him by rebelling against God and dragging him with her out of paradise. Then Eve bore fruit, and the daughters of Eve increased, till one of them, Mary, reversed the course of nature again by conceiving without a man; and whereas Eve became the mother of men, Mary the Virgin became the mother of God.

Who then, psychologically speaking, was Eve the tempted and the temptress, and who was Mary the untemptable? Eve the proud who brought disaster on mankind, and Mary the humble who brought salvation?

I cannot, I think, do better than begin by quoting on this subject from the remarkable sermon of St. Bernard called De Conversione[1], in which he describes the negative anima or what he calls the diseased "will" in terms of an internalised Eve, referring to her as "that lady" who "lies at home paralysed and grievously tormented" (p. 14) and who, when commanded by the reason to amend her ways, "leaps forth in her fury, forgetful of all her weakness. With dishevelled locks, and with torn garments, with naked breast, scrabbling at her ulcers, gnashing the teeth in her parched mouth, infecting the very air with her poisonous breath, she exclaims: Why is not the reason ashamed of such an attack, such an onslaught upon the wretched will? Is this, says she, all your conjugal fidelity? Is this the way you feel for me when I suffer so much?" (p. 15). And, having enumerated all her faults, he goes on "For it is thus

---

[1] The quotions are mode from the English translation by Watkin Williams: Of Conversion, a sermon to the clergy by Saint Bernard of Clairvaux, translated by Watkin Williams, London, 1938.

with the soul; as there is the memory which is befouled, so there is the will which befouls" (p. 17), and ends up "Reduce to meekness the wild motions of the will, and make it thy care to tame the cruel beast. Thou art bound to the will; strive to relax the bond which thou canst not break. The will is thy Eve..." (p. 19).

What then is the proud Eve, thus produced out of Adam's body, but the projection of the anima, bringing with it indeed children peopling the earth, for unregenerate nature cares not for the soul, but bringing at the same time all the ills that are described by the holy Father in this Rabelaisian manner which is so refreshingly different from the polite milk-and-water Christianity of modern times? On the contrary, the humble Mary brings forth no merely human children, but shows forth the Second Adam reborn phoenix-like out of the ashes of the First. Psychologically speaking, just as Eve is the anima, both in the flesh and as a negative projection in the personal unconscious, so Mary represents the wholly inwardised positive anima or mother-image in the impersonal unconscious.

For this, Mary pays the price according to Catholic doctrine of having no ordinary human children[1], nor even a human mate (for Catholic theology has it that Joseph also remained a virgin, whence his position of patron of celibate orders), while Eve, for her human mother-hood, pays the terrible price that both Genesis and St. Bernard describe.

---

[1] Christ's so-called ,,brothers" are taken to be ,,brothers" in the ,,classificatory" sense only, as described in the footnote on p. 271.

Divine incestuous union before the Fall

But the earth has to be peopled, or there would be no people to save, so Eve has her positive function as well as Mary. What their respective functions are in the psychology of man I now hope to show in anthropological terms through a study of the problem of Incest Taboo, which will be found to be very different indeed from that put forward by Freud and based on more exact anthropological data. For, in the Garden of Eden, Adam was as yet within the womb in blissful union with his mother and in the innocence which was also the ignorance resulting from lack of any contact with what is called the "world", given up to an uninterrupted contemplation of all the mysteries of creation, being himself the material embodiment of it and of its inner processes; a creature without pride not yet launched out into that ocean of affairs in which man must himself become biologically a creator and so suffer the temptation (which was Eve's, directly handed to her by the serpent) of thinking himself "like God", in other words of acquiring the imperious will which was Eve's and so landing himself in the condition of inflation which leads to outer darkness.

This state of one-ness with the mother while yet within her womb, typified by Adam and Eve in Eden, is the epitome of incestuous union with which all life begins, and also to which it must return, though on another plane. But between this alpha and omega, this beginning and this end, this First Paradise of Eden within the maternal womb and the Second Paradise of New Jerusalem within the womb of God, there lies a wilderness in which complete separation must be made from the first as sine qua non of entry into the second. And this wilderness is life, conscious and active life overhung by the shadow of death; in which the loneliness of the path of personal individuation is either shirked because the spiritual umbilical cord keeping a man tied to his earthly mother is never wholly cut, resulting in every kind of negative projection, or else this task is accepted to the best of a man's ability, whereby the union with the internal anima or positive mother-image is gradually formed, leading in turn to the soul's brideship with God to whom the anima herself acts as a bridge, thus leaving the individual free to conduct life without negative projections due to undue and unrealisable dependence on human love.

Basic nature of incest desire. Taboo not instituted on biological grounds, but is a sacrificial system with both manifest and latent content.

This inner conflict, common to all men, is reflected in the organisation of human society by the tremendous taboo placed on incest by primitive peoples — I say tremendous because it is, with them, a matter of life and death. All society is based on it, and without it no society would exist. Nevertheless the misconceptions in the modern mind about the real meaning of incest are so great that we are ourselves in danger of carrying on incestuous unions in the form of negative participations mystiques without knowing it; and, indeed, much neurosis is itself the result of such psychologically though not necessarily physically incestuous unions.

Freud says (it may be taken that this is the corner-stone of his teaching, and it is one which no serious psychotherapist would dispute) that the incest desire is fundamental in man. Thus, he says "Psychoanalysis has taught us that the first object selection of the boy is of an incestuous nature and that it is directed to the forbidden objects, the mother and the sister." (Totem and Taboo[1], p.28.) Further, "The basis of taboo is a forbidden action for which there exists a strong inclination in the unconscious" (ibid p. 54). He also says "The law only forbids men to do what their instincts incline them to do... Instead of assuming therefore, from the legal prohibition of the incest, that there is a natural aversion to incest we ought rather to assume that there is a natural instinct in favour of it" (ibid p. 205).

These statements, bold in their day, are now commonplaces of all psychological analysis. It is our task to ask ourselves why, if this desire is so imperious, such a taboo should ever have grown up.

The usual explanation, so usual that it is implicit in the thinking of almost every modern person and particularly of those calling themselves "scientific", is that it is due to the biologically harmful effects of in-breeding. This view, however, does not tally with the facts. Freud himself, referring to both men and animals, says "the harmful consequences of in-breeding are not established beyond all doubt even to-day and in man they can be shown only with difficulty" (ibid p. 206); and also "it must be pointed out that a prohibition against in-breeding as an element weakening to the race, which is imposed from practical hygienic motives, seems quite inadequate to explain the deep abhorrence which our society feels against incest" (ibid p. 207). This is so true that, apparently unknown to Freud but as I shall shortly show, one of the outstanding anthropological facts

[1] Sigmund Freud, Totem and Taboo, English translation by A. A. Brill, London, 1919.

is that, on the contrary, the incest taboo as practiced among most really primitive people is **not only designed to prevent in-breeding, but in many cases carries with it obligations that actually promote it.**

The first thing to be quite clear about is, therefore, that, contrary to all modern habits of thought and popular belief, in-breeding is not biologically harmful. If such a belief were true, it would be true also of animals, which it manifestly is not since all specialized and so-called "pure" breeds of animals are based on it. There are indeed cases, such as small isolated communities, in which Europeans are said to have become degenerate through in-breeding, but these are not proved and many other factors enter in such as extreme poverty which are very frequently ignored. There is, on the other hand, the positive evidence to the contrary of the innumerable isolated or semi-isolated communities in which in-breeding is not only practised but has continued to be practised for countless generations all over the world, not only to-day but also in the past, with no such negative results, but on the contrary those tribes which have practised it have been so strong as to have borne the whole brunt of primitive man's struggle to lay the foundations of civilisation, and to maintain these against all the disintegrating forces of nature.

If biological reasons were not the prime causes of the taboo, what was? Freud's hypothesis, as advanced in Totem and Taboo, is that of the primitive horde led by an aged patriarch who possessed all the women and whose sons finally rebelled, killed him, and married his wives, thus giving rise to the so-called Oedipus Complex. This has done more to discredit Freud among anthropologists than any of his works, since there is no evidence whatever that such a condition ever existed, and the misinterpretation of anthropological data on which it is based is well known. Incidentally, this purely subjective myth is a fascinating one when regarded as a reflexion of Freud's own psychology, and, taken symbolically, represents an unconscious rebellion against his own patriarchal and over-intellectualised attitude as represented by the father.

This is not to say that the Oedipus Complex does not exist, or that it does not hold a prominent place in the personal unconscious of modern man. But it is not found to anything like the same extent among the very primitive. Its formulation as a basic dogma of psychoanalysis appears to me to result from the view expressed in another of Freud's statements to the effect that "Taboo is a very primitive prohibition imposed from without (by an authority) and directed against the strongest desires of man" (ibid p. 59). That it is indeed directed against man's strongest desires is not in dispute, but that it is imposed ultimately from without I should dispute strongly, since analytical psychology can demonstrate from dream material that the ultimate source of the taboo lies within and is a dictate not of the personal unconscious but of the deeper levels of the collective unconscious, and only has to be enforced from without (i. e. by the collective conscious) when the deep inner sacrificial truths mentioned below are lost sight of.

I have risked tiring the reader by quoting these well-known passages in order to show just how far we can go with Freud, and where we part from him. For, to him, the ultimate authority appears to be external, whereas for us it is internal. We know that the ambivalence found in the psyche may not be solely due to external causes nor to be essentially negative at all, but is to be found deep down in the very nature of life and as the very mainspring of our being, becoming negative only if thwarted by us, but being in the nature of illumination if it is not. For the maxim that nothing exists outwardly that did not previously exist internally is fundamental to Jung's teaching.

If, then, the authority imposing the taboo is internal: What is it, and Why is it? The answer requires a teleological understanding, not an aetiological one. Aetiologically every kind of reason could be adduced, as every neurotic adduces aetiological rationalisations for all the ills that have befallen him, but the wise analyst seeks the reason not in the past but in the purpose, assuming that every ill is due to a misunderstanding of that purpose.

For the ultimate purpose of everything in life is always sacrifice, which means transformation, the transformation of something "natural" into that which is "supernatural", that is to say not less but still more natural than biological nature because on a "higher", or as we should say "deeper", level. For there is nothing in nature that is not there in order to be transformed, and it is a universal phenomenon that the "natural", which always starts off by being "good", inevitably becomes regarded as "bad" if or when it does not submit to transformation. That is why the Latin word sacer, from which our "sacrifice" is derived, like its Polynesian equivalent "taboo" carries with it the double connotation of "unclean" and „holy", indicating the "uncleanliness" of that which resists transformation and the "holiness" of that which is transformed. Freud recognises the ambivalence of the concept (queer only to the modern mind but fundamental to the primitive), but curiously enough misses its import. For the fundamental meaning both of sacer and of "taboo" is "set apart", and what is set apart is regarded as "unclean" only by those who do not understand the meaning of transformation, but is recognised as being "holy" by those who do. For every instinct has to be satisfied, but there are two spheres, those of the flesh and of the spirit, which are complementary opposites in the sense that what is forbidden and indeed may be deadly in the flesh can and must be satisfied in the spirit, so that, in the words of the gospel, "all things may be fulfilled".

Jung treats the question with regard to the incest wish, not, as Freud does, by saying that the desire for the mother on the part of the adult is a negative thing that has to be avoided, but that on the contrary it is a positive thing that has to be followed up at all costs until its meaning becomes clear and it can therefore be re-integrated as a positive spiritual factor into conscious life.

We are now in a position to turn to primitive man, and to ask ourselves the following questions:

1. If incest is not biologically harmful, in what way is it so harmful that primitive man regards it as a cardinal sin?
2. This being the case, why, after forbidding marriage between a man and his mother, sister or daughter, do the prohibitions against lesser degrees of incest vary so greatly from place to place, and why should many primitive peoples not only permit but actually insist (as I shall show) on marriage between first cousins?
3. Why, after all this apparent care against in-breeding, should there be special religious occasions set apart in which, as sometimes happens, all these regulations are suspended and complete licence allowed?

4. Why, when ordinary men and women live normally under this strict and mortal taboo, should the gods they worship and the culture-heroes they admire and hold up as patterns of life, so very frequently (and especially where the taboo is strongest) be believed to have married their mothers, sisters or daughters?

The answer is, in the first place, that the taboo is not directed against in-breeding, but arises from reasons of quite a different kind, which will be seen to explain all these apparent anomalies and show that they are not only not anomalies but follow logically from what its purpose is.

2.
MANIFEST PURPOSE OF THE TABOO: THE "ANIMA WITHOUT", LEADING TO THE EXPANSION OF SOCIETY

The purpose of the incest taboo has, as I have already mentioned, a manifest aspect, and a latent one.

To take the former first, its manifest purpose is "civilisation" in its most literal sense, that is to say, the enabling of men to live together in amity and in a condition of mutual co-operation.

Systematised in-breeding among Australian tribes. "Cellular" or "closed" kinship systems.

To illustrate this, I propose briefly to examine the known and carefully tabulated facts concerning some of the tribes on the Australian continent. These tribes, or hordes as they are called, for they are mostly food-gatherers often restricted to less than 200 members, have a social organisation of great apparent complexity, rigorously enforced through the action of age-long public opinion, the expression and conservation of which rests with the older members of the tribe. This unofficial and unformulated governmental power of the older men is of greater importance than is usually understood. For we are ourselves so used to quick changes in the social system brought about partly by the huge size and manifold interests of modern communities, changes often imposed from above or through the action of outstanding personalities, that we find it difficult to conceive of their absence. In primitive communities all these factors are absent. The social horizon is restricted to a few hundreds of people and has been so for countless centuries. There are no chiefs to wield arbitrary authority, nor do the extremely limited possibilities allow of the emergence of anything in the nature of what we now call "reformers". Indeed, as I have emphasised in another work[1], a really primitive community resembles an individual person in the sense that its members are all one. They are in the first place all closely related to one another, so that the action of one has immediate repercussions on all the others, and in the second place the solidarity of these tiny groups in the face of natural forces as well as enemy tribes is of such over-riding importance that any major departure from the accepted order is highly dangerous to the delicate balance on which the whole tiny structure depends, and is therefore punishable by death. This balance may be compared not only to the external balance of the human frame but to its internal balance also, the balance of glandular secretions or the structure of cells.

[1] John Layard, Stone Men of Malekula, London 1942, pp. 102, 115 ff., 593.

Indeed, the "cellular" analogy is such a close one that, as will shortly be shown, the social organisation of Australian tribes is, like that in many parts of the world, based on a primary division into two moieties which split first into four, then into eight sections (and elsewhere into six or twelve) in a manner closely similar on the one hand to that of primitive biological organisms, and on the other hand to the sub-divisions of the individual psyche[1], and the smooth interaction of all these interlocking parts is essential to the survival of the tribe.

I therefore propose first to examine the origin of the cellular organisation itself, in order then to demonstrate the gradual emergence of the social (that is to say the manifest) organism out of the biological, and then how in its turn the social aspect inevitably gives rise to the latent spiritual or psychological aspect.

But before proceeding with this I must once more make it quite plain that, with regard to the incest taboo, in all probability neither the ultimate social aspect nor yet (and this is quite certain) the ultimate psychological aspect is present in the minds of the natives, or at least to the rank and file. The typical misconception that man rules his own destiny (in the vulgar sense of knowing with any kind of exactness what he is doing) is to be seen in the opening pages of Freud's study where, discussing the apparently complicated regulations associated with the taboo, he says that they "seem to spring from legislation with a definite aim in view"[2]. In the first place such a concept as legislation, which is the result of definite planning, is utterly foreign to the primitive mind. And in the second,

---
[1] See page 276 of this article.
[2] Freud, Totem and Taboo, p. 14.

following from it, it cannot be emphasised too strongly that the forces which rule men's lives are not conscious in this kind of way, that man is not "captain of his fate" but that he is, on the contrary, part of a scheme of growth and development of which, since he is part of it, he cannot know the end, and which of its own power forces him to find out by a ceaseless process of trial and error what is the path that he is meant to tread. Further, that this path is never revealed to him in direct terms, but always under the appearance of material fact concealing a spiritual purpose behind the prompting on the material plane.

To take the former or material plane first, envisage man the animal, or, more important still, woman the animal, guarding her brood against all comers, jealous and murderous against any who should approach them, her mate providing the food and aiding in the defence. No social life could come of that. The brood grows up. Either the boys, after the "gang" stage, return and mate with her or with their sisters, or else they start other families with strange females who will be equally hostile in defence of theirs.

No human beings are known to live like this, for no human beings live without some kind of social life, and for social life two things are necessary.

It is not enough to rear children and defend them until they are old enough to defend themselves. There must be co-operation as well as defence. The easiest form of co-operation would clearly be within the family unit itself, through in-breeding which is not biologically unsound. But in-breeding has one effect, often thought to be biological but really cultural, namely that not only does no new blood enter the family, but also no new thoughts. Methods of food-gathering will be stereotyped, as also will methods, if any there be at this stage, of providing the shelter so necessary for any cultural advance. Culture-contact is essential to progress. But so also is a measure of peace. Therefore "new blood" must be brought in, not for the sake of the physical "blood", but for the pooling of new experience based on a common need. But it must be "new blood" which is not hostile. And as all primitive life is based on kinship the new mate must be

(a) unrelated for the sake of the pooled experience, and yet
(b) related for the sake of peace.

Marriage with the mother's brother's daughter.

How can such a paradoxical demand be fulfilled? To the primitive mind there is no paradox, for every man has two parents, but under very primitive conditions in which knowledge of physiological paternity may be entirely lacking there is only one obvious parent demonstrable by means of the senses, and that is the mother from whom the child was born. Therefore, when seeking for a mate, a man does not take any woman from any unrelated group (such a practice is almost unknown), but, on the contrary, he goes (or did in early days almost all over the world) to his natural protector, that is to say not to his father who in matrilineal communities is often only a visitor, but to his mother's brother, and says "Uncle, will you give me a wife?" And Uncle says: "Why, yes, you can have my daughter", whereupon he marries his mother's brothers's daughter, who is his first cousin on his mother's side[1].

---

[1] John Layard, Stone Men of Malekula, p. 103. With regard to this and other marriages with specific relatives mentioned below, it may be objected that such a relative might not exist. As explained in detail on p. 99 of that work, however,

This arrangement fulfils both conditions. For the wife, who brings in the new blood, is in terms of kinship, both related to him on his mothers side, which means peace and family solidarity, and at the same time is not immediately related to him on his fathers side and thus brings to his family unit the new trains of thought and experience which she has derived from hers.

It thus becomes not only permissible but, as the resulting social organizations become stabilised, also obligatory over a large part of the world's surface, for a man to marry his mother's brother's daughter or first cousin on his mother's side; and this is to-day, and has been for countless centuries, the prescribed marriage in most parts of Australia and in innumerable other parts of the world. In biblical times it was the marriage which Isaac (Gen. 28, 2) commanded Jacob to make with the daughters of Laban, his mother's brother, of whom Rachel the younger was his beloved and gave birth to Joseph; and, as though to emphasise the divinely incestuous nature of this union, on Laban's meeting with Jacob the latter is expressly referred to as his sister's son, and Laban exclaims "Surely thou art my bone and my flesh" (Gen. 29. 13, 14). But at the same time the second condition of acquiring new experience was also fullfilled, since Laban "lived in a far country", whither Jacob had to go and work for Rachel for fourteen years before Laban consented to their union. For real incest is of the mind, not of the body, and the purpose of the incest taboo is to prevent a negative participation mystique,

---

almost all primitive kinship systems are organised on a so-called „classificatory" principle by means of which certain collateral relatives are classed together in such a way that, for example, in an overtly matrilineal community the mother's sister's son is for sociological purposes called „brother". If, then, a man's mother has no brother with a suitable daughter for him to marry, one of her classificatory brothers will provide his daughter instead.

which is not of the blood but of the spirit. Every man nowa-days who has, as we figuratively put it, "married his mother" has contracted an incestuous union though there may be no blood relationship between him and his wife, but in spite of this we pride ourselves that we are not incestuous because we don't marry our sisters, nor yet, with rare exceptions, our cousins; though here it must be added that this latter reference is to town-dwellers only, since healthy country stock in small village communities everywhere were, until the advent of strangers due to improved communications, to a very large extent in-bred.

However this may be with regard to Europe, it is the case that marriage with the mother's brother's daughter, that is to say with the first cousin on the mother's side, is and has been the basic form of marriage for countless centuries for at least a third of the world's population.

Dual Organization and the 4-section kinship-system

But this is not all. For, among many people, the degree of consanguinity prescribed between married people has been still greater in some once wide-spread cases, in a manner which I will now describe. For, while among certain peoples this system based on each man marrying his first cousin on the mother's side has not been what is called a "closed" or circumscribed one, that is to say that it spread outwards, in the sense that the wife's brother, while himself also marrying his mother's brother's daughter, found her in another group, in other cases this form of marriage was combined with what is called the Dual Organization of Society into two exogamous matrilineal moieties, to one of which every member of the tribe belongs and from the other of which he must take his wife. These moieties are themselves highly symbolical of the fundamental dichotomy both of external nature and of internal psychological structure as mirrored in the social organisation of the tribe, as may be seen from the names by which they are known. Hocart[1] thus lists the pairs of moieties in such widely separated areas as Australia, Melanesia, South India, North and Central America, Siberia and Ancient India (and many other areas might have been cited), in all of which almost exactly similar contrasting names for the two moieties are used, such as: — Light and Dark, Sky and Earth, Day and Night, Seaward and Landward, Noble and Lower, Big and Little, Right and Left, Gentle and Rough, and Male and Female (despite the fact that each moiety is made up of both sexes), and in which, though the prescribed inter-marriages preclude the possibility of special characteristics inherited through the blood, nevertheless the members of the two moieties are held to be recognisable respectively by the contrasting character-traits symbolised by their complementary-opposite names. Now, all native transactions, whether of barter or in the presentation of food, goods or ritual courtesies or any other things, are characterised by the equality of exchange, and the more primitive the community the more exact the correspondence in kind. This also applies to marriage, giving rise to what is called sister-exchange marriage whereby when a man marries a wife he gives in exchange his own sister to be married to this wife's brother.

Now, in a kinship system based on the Dual Organization in which each man marries his mother's brother's daughter

[1] A. M. Hocart, Kings and Councillors, Cairo, 1936, pp. 273–277.

and also gives his sister to be married to his wife's brother, and where this double transaction is repeated from generation to generation, the very important result automatically occurs that the wife, who is on the one hand the mother's brother's daughter, is on the other hand also the father's sister's daughter, thus:

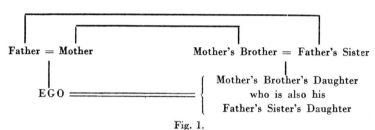

Fig. 1.
To illustrate "cross-cousin" marriage

In other words, in such a system, each man marries his first cousin not only on his mother's side but also on his father's, so that the incest-at-one-remove is doubled.

There is no space here to elaborate on all the implications of such a system, and I can only refer the reader to my book Stone Men of Malekula chapter V, in which it is shown that in Australia, despite the overt patrilineal organization of individual hordes and the great distances and innumerable linguistic barriers that divide them, the matrilineal moieties in fact cover the whole continent and form the fundamental bond underlying the whole kinship structure. The effect of this customary form of marriage repeated over countless generations is, in each horde that practices it, the automatic formation of two patrilineal moieties also. And these patrilineal moieties cross with the matrilineal moieties in such a way as to create locally (as for instance

THE INCEST TABOO AND THE VIRGIN ARCHETYPE

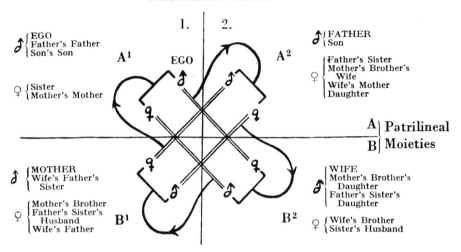

Fig. 2.
4-Section Kinship System.
Matrilineal moieties in vertical columns 1 and 2. Patrilineal moieties in horizontal columns A and B. Each of the four quarters so formed represents a marriage section. Male and female signs ♂ and ♀ represent *all* men and women in a given section, in which each man marries his MBD who belongs to the opposite matrilineal moiety *and* to the opposite patrilineal moiety from himself. Curved descent lines lead from each marriage to the children of that marriage, who belong to the matrilineal moiety of the mother and to the patrilineal moiety of the father. Thus a man of A^1 marries a woman of B^2 and their children are A^2, but his sister's children are B^1.
(From *Stone Men of Malekula*, Fig. 20, with kind permission of Messrs. Chatto and Windus.)

among the Kariera in West Australia) what is called a 4-section kinship system, a kind of primitive "cellular" organism which is at one and the same time endogamous in that it is completely self-contained, and also exogamous in that no man ever marries a woman who belongs either to his own continent-wide matrilineal moiety or to his own local patrilineal moiety.

This is the simplest of so-called "closed" kinship systems, of which the diagram page 275 is a schematic representation.

Although it may seem complicated to us, it is very simple to the native, and while for an adequate explanation of it I must refer the reader to the above-mentioned work, it will be seen that the diagram does in fact include all possible relationships, and, which is vital from the native point of view, shows how the entire population of the horde (which it must be remembered may not number more than 200 members) falls into four groups or sections, from only one of which (that containing his mother's brother's children) a man is allowed to select his bride.

To those of us who think in terms of internal psychic attitudes corresponding to external relationships, the implications of this "cellular" social organism interpreted in terms of the psychological structure of each individual composing it will be seen to be very great. To take one instance only, I may point out in passing how the four chief figures in the psychological drama of life, namely Ego, his Mother, his Father and his Wife, all fall into different sections, and that a preliminary discussion of these in terms of the four psychological functions will be found in an article entitled "Primitive Kinship as mirrored in the Psychological structure of Modern Man" (British Journal of Medical Psychology. Vol. XX, Part 2, 1944 pp. 118–134).

Expansion beyond the limits of the 4-section system.

If the above brief account has any lesson to teach, it will be that the prevention of biological in-breeding as such is very definitely not the reason for the incest taboo, but that, on the contrary, its object is the expansion not of biological but of social contacts. That is to say that, by forcing a man to marry outside the immediate circle of his own biological family unit, he is thereby brought into contact with a wider group of related persons all having mutual obligations towards one another and therefore pooling their diverse experiences and discoveries, as well as building up a primitive social unit for purposes of mutual protection and the solidarity of the group.

So far, however, the group thus achieved is a very small one. For what countless ages it remained on this secure but limited basis we do not know. The next phase, so far as Australia was concerned, consisted in doubling its size. But it must not be supposed that any primitive community did this "on purpose". Till man can find some way of discovering what nature intends him to do and of doing it in a straightforward way, the means by which advances are made will continue to be by way of quarrels about what seem essentials but are in fact only means to an end. The best explanation so far put forward as to the social mechanism by which this new advance was made is that suggested by Professor Radcliffe-Brown who puts it down to the age-long problem of the mother-in-law, taking in this case the form of the extreme awkwardness, which the 4-section system entails, of a man's wife's mother being at the same time his father's sister. Now, among the rules of avoidance that accompany the incest taboo is that which prohibits a man from speaking to, or having any direct communication with, his wife's mother, since she belongs to one of those categories of women with whom there is a temptation to mate, but with whom at no cost must this be allowed to happen. But if the wife's mother is at the same time the father's sister, in a patrilineal community such as the Australian horde, she is, until marriage, a member of Ego's own camp, and even after her marriage is a frequent visitor to it. The problem then becomes, how to find a wife who can still be reckoned as a kind of "mother's brother's daughter", but does not bring with her this very awkward problem.

The solution[1] actually found is that a man, instead of marrying his first cousin on his mother's side, marries his second cousin on that side instead; in other words, instead of marrying his mother's brother's daughter, he marries his mother's mother's brother's daughter's daughter. This effectively removes the embarrasing situation I have mentioned, since this relative's mother is no longer necessarily also the father's sister. This is the manifest reason for the alteration in custom. But the latent reason (and therefore the ultimate cause) is that it brings about an enlargement of the whole social system, and actually (as described on page 116 of my above-mentioned book) causes each of the patrilineal moieties to split, thus giving rise to four patrilineal descent groups instead of two, which, combining with the two matrilineal moieties which remain constant, lead to the expansion of the former 4-section system into an 8-section one. This is the system which has been most thoroughly investigated among the Aranda of Central Australia. In this expanded system the

[1] For a more detailed exposition of this, see my Stone Men of Malekula, p. 116.

incest barrier is also extended, and marriage with the mother's brother's daughter which in a 4-section system was not only allowed but prescribed, now becomes looked on as being as incestuous as intercourse with the mother or sister, and not only marriage but any kind of relationship with her is punishable by death.

Elsewhere, as in parts of Melanesia, it is the mother's brother's daughter's daughter who becomes the prescribed bride producing a 6-section system, and there is evidence that in the Chou period in China the system had expanded into a 12-section one[1].

It is, incidentally, of interest to note that every "closed" system of this kind is a repetitive one. Thus, in a 4-section system such as has been depicted in Fig. 2, while a man's children must inevitably belong to a different section from his own, his sons' sons return to his own section every two generations. This rotation of what are called "sociological equivalences" varies, however, with the characteristics of particular systems. For example, in a 6-section system formed of two matrilineal moieties and three patrilineal trisections such as that of Ranon in the New Hebrides, while those in the direct male line of descent return to the same kinship section every two generations so that a man calls his father's father and son's sons "brother", those in the direct female line of descent take three generations to complete the cycle so that it is the mother's mother's mother and for a woman her daughter's daughter's daughters who in this case are called "sister" (see Fig. 3).

Similarly, in a 12-section system such as that found in the Chou period in China, which is based on two patrilineal moieties and six matrilineal descent groups, the cycle

[1] Ibid, p. 151.

280   JOHN LAYARD

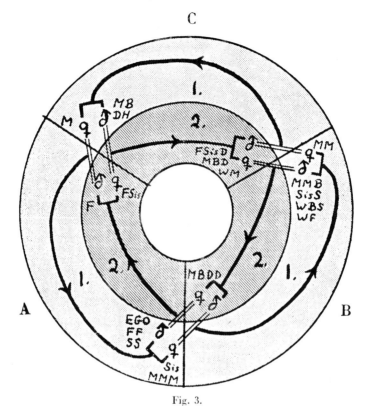

Fig. 3.

6-Section System. Functional Diagram ♂ = MBDD.

Matrilineal moieties represented by circular bands 1 and 2.

Radial lines divide the three patrilineal trisections A, B and C.

(From *Stone Men of Malekula*, Fig. 27, with kind permission of Messrs. Chatto and Windus.)

This diagram depicts the kinship system of Ranon in the island of Ambrim situated in the New Hebrides archipelago of Melanesia, where each man marries his mother's brother's daughter's daughter. This system repeats itself every 2 generations in the male line and every 3 generations in the female line, so that a man calls his father's father "brother" and his mother's mother's mother "sister".

takes 6 generations to repeat itself in the direct male line
in such a way that it is the son's son's son's son's son's son's
sons who falls into the category of "brothers". Thus each
such "closed" kinship system, returning upon itself every
so many generations, assumes the configuration of a human
mandala divided into 4, 6, 8 or 12 sections, one of which
is figured here and yet others are to be found depicted in
Chapters V and VI of the above-mentioned work.

So far as is known, the 12-section system forms the uttermost limit to which such "closed" or "circular" kinship
systems have been developed, and, by the time this stage
is reached, the manifest object of the incest taboo in expanding society having been thus achieved[1], it falls to pieces
and subsequently the very size of society itself, with its
numerous opportunities, assures varied contact to such an
extent that all these complicated taboos are no longer
necessary and there remains among us to-day only the basic
one prohibiting marriage with members of the biological
family unit.

3.

LATENT OR INNER PURPOSE OF THE TABOO; THE REALISATION OF THE "ANIMA WITHIN"

Having now traced the external development of the
anima-problem, for such it is, with its fulfilment in terms
of mating with an actual spouse, what now of its inner
development which must be of a complementary opposite
nature, for, as the sexual desire towards the mother or

---
[1] In other parts of the world the expansion is achieved by unilateral methods,
whether matrilineal or patrilineal, or else by a mixture of both in varying degrees.

sister recedes from consciousness, so must it inevitably increase as a psychological or spiritual longing.

I take it as axiomatic — and this lies I think at the root of all religion — that every instinctive desire must ultimately be satisfied, and that what therefore cannot be satisfied in the flesh must be satisfied in the spirit. This is where the whole Freudian rejection of spiritual values breaks down. Freud is honest enough, on page 247 of his Totem and Taboo, after his exposition of the Oedipus Complex and the consequent rise of male deities, to say: — "In this evolution I am at a loss to indicate the place of the great maternal deities, who perhaps everywhere precede the paternal deities." This, I submit, is where Analytical Psychology comes in, and where true religion of a properly balanced kind comes in also. For, in the life of the individual, the incest taboo produces the following results. In the first place it forces the external search for the fulfilment of the mating instinct to reach out beyond its primary object within the biological family unit towards a more distant object with a view to enlarging the social and experiential horizon. But the repressed primary (incestuous) longings still exist, so that to the desire for the new mate is also added the disappointment that she is not all that is desired. And thus the second factor arises, namely that of the projection of the unfulfilled part of the desire, which acquires a negative and a positive aspect, of which the negative is always the first to become apparent, since, as in the case of the movement from a 4-section towards an 8-section system described above, it is the dissatisfaction which is always the spur to effort.

Thus we get, on the one hand, the negative attitude

towards women and their consequent degradation in the social scale that is so characteristic of early patrilineal societies, coupled in the mythological sphere with the belief in a Devouring Earth Mother who, outraged by the treatment meted out to her sex, spends her time demanding blood-sacrifices of all kinds[1].

On the other hand we get the positive aspect of fulfilment on the religious level in three ways: — firstly in those "sacred orgies" to which Freud refers "in which persons of just these forbidden degrees of kinship seek sexual union" (Totem and Taboo, page 18), thus demonstrating once more that biological in-breeding is not the purpose of the incest taboo; secondly in the almost universal belief at this cultural level that gods and culture-heroes in fact do just what men under normal circumstances are so cruelly forbidden to do, that is to say, break every incest taboo and mate with their mothers or sisters; and thirdly in the emergence of divine kings whose duty (as in Egypt and elsewhere) it was to marry their sisters.

In this way the primary desire is fulfilled either by men themselves when under special religious licence to do so, that is when they themselves perform the "sacred marriage", or else in phantasy when the desire for this sacred incestuous marriage is projected upon the gods. It is to be noted, however, that even among the gods and culture heroes the union is rarely with the most primary object of all, which is the mother, but more usually with the sister who is herself secondary to the mother.

These unions are as a rule accompanied by miraculous or

---

[1] A brief discussion of the Female Devouring Monster as compensating in the unconscious for the inferior position given to woman in the conscious will be found in Stone Men of Malekula, pp. 219 ff.

unusual events all of which are highly symbolical, as when
Erets, culture hero of the small island of Atchin in the New
Hebrides where I have worked, courted his sister Le-rets
(note the similarity of name) by floating a kite over the
channel which divided their habitations until it reached her
house (where she was of course married in the flesh to
another man), and to the kite he had attached a fowl which,
by its crowing, made her look up and receive the message.
The channel actually exists, but is, of course, symbolic of
the division between the spiritual and material worlds.
Birds everywhere signify spirit, and rope or string (in this
case holding the kite) always signifies the union of conscious
with unconscious, in other words, the sure but thin thread
of spiritual intuition; and the cock, as everyone knows,
signifies the dawn, in other words, the gateway into the
unconscious, its crowing being the signal announcing the
passage from one sphere into the other, like that of the
cock which crew three times during the Passion.

Internalisation through Sacrifice.
The Psychology of Celibacy.

We have seen how the social or manifest purpose of
the incest taboo is to enlarge the social horizon. We now
see how its latent or spiritual purpose is to enlarge the
spiritual horizon by developing the idea that there is after
all a sphere in which the primary desire may be satisfied,
namely the divine sphere of the gods together with that
of their semi-divine counterparts, the culture heroes.

This is however not all, for these are mythological projections, and, satisfying as they may be on this level, they
do not achieve for man the ultimate spiritual union. This

can be done only by sacrifice. The incest taboo is itself a sacrifice, but by no means a complete one, since the manifest purpose of the taboo is social only, and its spiritual aspect is not yet realised. The latent purpose of it on the spiritual level is achieved fully only when the taboo has been pushed to its uttermost and includes all women, that is to say with the advent of celibacy as a definite technique by means of which union with the divine can be achieved.

This raises the the problem of celibate priests who come for psychological treatment because, for reasons unknown to them, they are inhibited in the conduct of their religious duties. It might by some be wrongly supposed that, when it came to the sexual aspect of their problems, ordinary analytical methods might be inapplicable to them on account of their ideal of celibacy and its enforcement by an authoritarian system. Experience shows, however, that psychological concepts regarding the release of libidinous matter not only apply to them quite as much as to the ordinary layman, but are applicable if possible even more, since true celibacy, far from being an affair of sex-repression, is itself, if rightly understood, the most complete expression of the transformed sex instinct. It is in fact the case that sex-repression in any form hinders the celibate even more than it hinders the married man. For what the celibate is seeking is deeper than sex, that is to say a direct union with "the other" which is God. But, since he is human and endowed with sex instinct without which he would be as nothing, and since individuation of any kind demands the fullest development of all desire, if sex desire is repressed the way to God is to that extent blocked also, and cannot be found until the unconscious inhibition is removed. This is so vital to the priesthood that it is astonishing how frequently it is overlooked. But the analysis of priests shows that it is the case, and that the sex instinct, far from being feared, has actually to be heightened to such a pitch that it bursts through the barriers of flesh and reaches the depths – or heights – which give access to the divine, bringing about a union formed not of flesh but of the spirit. And thus the incest taboo reaches its final goal, which is the anima within, divested of all projection in the form of fleshly desire upon the anima without.

Thus, to those not acquainted with monasticism, it comes sometimes as a surprise to learn that the monks' chief search was love, and that for example St. Bernard, the greatest of all Cistercians (who shut themselves off from the world and maintain the rule of almost complete silence) when addressing his monks as abbot used as his main text the Song of Songs, which is the most outstandingly sexual poem in Holy Writ. All mystical literature also is based on sexual imagery such as the Church being the Bride, and Christ the Bridegroom.

But, unlike the pagan gods and culture heroes who married their sisters, Christ had no sister. He only had a Mother, and in the cult of and mystical union with Our Lady which is so intimately bound up with all monastic life the incestuous cycle becomes complete, since we are Christ's mystical body and the Mother is the first (though not the ultimate) object of our desire, the fulfilment of which, as it is our duty to avoid in the flesh so it is our soul's health to seek in the spirit.

Thus our following-out of the implications of the incest taboo have led us along the same road as the biblical one, which starts with Eve being born out of Adam's side, that is to say the creation of desire and of the anima-image.

So long as Adam and Eve obeyed God in Eden there was no trouble, but there were also no children and no contact with the world outside. That is to say that they were "innocent", a state only possible within the womb and so long as mother and son are one. Man and the great Earth Mother were as yet unseparated. As Isaiah, fortelling the return to this blissful state says in chapter 62, verses 4–5, "Thy land shall be married. For as a young man marrieth a virgin, so shall thy sons marry thee". The meaning of virginity will be returned to shortly. What is of importance here is the spiritual union between son and mother, which is the beginning and the end of the anima problem. But Eve rebelled, and she and Adam were cast out. That is to say that mankind as we know it was born. The divine and innocent incestuous union was broken. Henceforth Adam could not find his anima within himself, but had to seek her externally in the form of a wife. Now children came. Eve became "the mother of all living", but at the same time she had to suffer. And she suffered not only through the labour of childbirth – "in sorrow shalt thou bring forth children" – but also through the negative projections of Adam, who had followed her advice in seeking to put himself on a level with God, and through it had found himself cast out of Paradise. This may be equated with the age of the inferior status of women and the rise of the Devouring Goddesses. Adam's desire was towards Eve, but she disappointed him, and the desire being the will, we get that devastating picture of thwarted desire painted by St. Bernard in the passage quoted at the beginning of this essay, ending with "the will is thy Eve", the negative anima at its worst.

Then comes the revelation of the solution, Mary the

Second Eve, who is the mother of the Second Adam, our Lord, who is Himself at the same time, in the tradition of the Church, her Spouse. But this time the mother was a Virgin, not the "mother of all living" as was Eve, but the mother of Him who Died. What is, then, the psychological meaning of Virginity?

4.

VIRGINITY

Virginity as spiritual pregnancy

Much has been written on this subject, and most readers of this essay will be familiar with Esther Harding's work on Women's Mysteries[1] during the course of which she demonstrates the psychological meaning of "virginity" as symbolising a re-creative submission to the demands of instinct. There is no space in an essay of this size to do more than call attention to this remarkable work. To quote at length from the innumerable instances of Virgin Goddesses of Fertility which she cites in support of this thesis would be redundant, since they can be read in her book. So, since the plan of this essay is the much simpler one of tracing the history of the incest taboo in terms of the transformation of instinctive values into spiritual ones with reference first to the anthropological data and then to the traditional contrast between Eve and Mary, I propose not to weary the reader by quoting directly from her in the text, but to proceed along the lines previously laid down

---

[1] M. Esther Harding, Womens's Mysteries, ancient and modern, Longmans Green, first English edition, London, 1935.

in this essay which are largely based on the results of clinical observations, and, to end up with an account of two dreams illustrating what has been said, confining myself to making a few relevant quotations from her book in footnotes in order to show, in certain places where our subject-matter coincides, the striking similarity between the conclusions we both have reached.

In the first place, though we now think of the word "virgin" as being synonymous with "chaste", this was not the case either with the Greek word parthenos or with the Hebrew 'almah of which "virgin" is the most usual biblical translation. For the Greek word was used of an unmarried girl whether she was chaste or not, and was in fact also applied to unmarried mothers. The Hebrew word means likewise "unmarried" without reference to premarital chastity. Thus in both cases the criterion for judging whether a woman were what is translated "virgin" or not was not whether she was chaste or unchaste (which is a biological criterion) but whether she were unmarried or married (which is on the contrary a purely legal one)[1]. The dividing line was thus not one having to do with nature (which is divine, having been created by God) but with law (which is not divine, having been created by man).

This would appear at first sight to present us with an insoluble paradox, particularly because it is of the essence of Christianity to consider Our Lady chaste. This was, however, also the belief in classical and pre-classical times with regard to other mothers of divine heroes, though in these cases the "virginity" carried with it the supposition

[1] Compare Harding, op. cit., pp. 76 and 79, in which she describes the real meaning of „virgin" as contrasting with „married". The Latin virgo similarly meant simply „unmarried" without reference to chastity, as is shown by the phrase virgo intacta used for a chaste woman.

that the mother had been impregnated by a god. Similarly, Our Lady is said to have "conceived by the Holy Ghost." It is, however, not by chance that she conceived before she married, for, as we have seen, what the ancients meant by the words which we translate "virginity", was not chastity but the absence of legal marriage. Indeed, it would appear that to be a virgin in the mythological sense the woman must conceive outside or before the marriage bond. Thus, had Our Lady been married at the time when she conceived she would no longer have been a virgin, and virginity is an essential attribute of the Mother of God[1].

What then do we mean by "virgin"? It may help us to examine those ways in which we use the word which are not directly concerned with sex. We speak of a "virgin forest" as being one in which the powers of nature are untrammelled and untouched by man. But we can think of this from two diametrically opposite points of view. We can think of it either from the view of the agricultural pioneer, who would regard it as something to be destroyed and uprooted as soon as possible; or else we can think of it from the point of view of a nature lover who would regard the virgin forest with awe as a supreme manifestation of pregnant nature, and who would oppose all the most enlightened efforts of the agriculturalist or town-builder to destroy its primitive beauty, — who would, in fact, treat it as inviolably holy. The one would represent "law and order" and the other "nature". So that we have here two opposite principles, both valid, the law of man in apparently open conflict with the law of God. Yet it is the law of God, the untrammelled law of pregnant though as yet

---

[1] See Harding, op. cit., p. 76, referring to pre-Christian times in which the Great Mother was always a „Virgin".

chaotic nature that we dub "virgin", and it is the reduction of that chaos which we call Law and Order.

Thus in this sense the word "virgin" does not mean chastity but the reverse, the pregnancy of nature, free and uncontrolled, corresponding on the human plane to unmarried love, in contrast to controlled nature corresponding to married love, despite the fact that from the legal point of view sexual intercourse within the marriage bond in the only kind which is regarded as "chaste"[1].

It will be seen that this argument has landed us in the midst of a paradox, a paradox only to be solved either a) by regarding the whole biblical story of the Virgin Birth as purely allegorical, which the Church asserts it is not, it being, as she maintains, a unique historical event; or else b) by reconciling the two through the realisation that instinct wants to be transformed into spirit, and that the Virgin Birth is the supreme example of this having been achieved, that is to say that Our Lady's womanhood was so complete and so closely united with God that it became self-reproductive.

For what woman, in her inmost soul, would not like to give birth to a man child without all the bother of having a husband, a child with whom she might be in complete unity of spirit without any outside interference? Many married women in fact do reach out towards this solution, but in a condition of negative participation mystique due to a largely unconscious relationship with the husband owing to a mixture of fear and pride, leading to a spiritually in-

---

[1] See Harding, op. cit., p. 76, quoting Frazer's remarks on Artemis as „a goddess of fertility though not of wedlock" and on „her constant identification with the unmarried but not chaste Asiatic goddesses of fertility"; and p. 77 regarding Ishtar as „not the exclusive wife of any male god" but „nevertheless referred to constantly as ‚the Virgin'"; also p. 78 with references to Aphrodite as „virgin", Demeter „who execrated marriage", and many others.

cestuous relationship with the son. But the archetypal conception of Mary is, on the contrary, that she was so humbly receptive in herself that she was a fitting mate for the All Highest in the form of the Holy Ghost. That is to say that she was so virginal (i. e. uncontaminated by man's misconceptions) as to be worthy of this honour and of receiving of the heavenly spiritual semen direct without its having to pass through the body of an imperfect man.

For all man-made law is negative. The laws of marriage can never create children, they can, if observed, only prevent children from being born in an undesired way. The positive factor is instinct, and the negative factor of law acts as an inhibition against untrammelled instinct for the sake of coupling with it spiritual values.

This brings us back to the whole question of the repression versus the transformation of sex. Women who have repressed their sex do often in fact become barren. Such is the case often in America today and to a less extent in Western Europe. Women in some parts of Southern India have a remedy for this which is "miraculous" in the same sense as, though in a lesser degree than, the Virgin Birth. For here the creator god Shiva is represented in his temples by a stone phallus called lingam standing in a stone basin, which is a female symbol, thus representing the divine union; a divine union, be it noted, not on the biological level (for a phallus is not made of flesh) but on the spiritual. If a married woman, though having concourse with her husband, remains barren, she has resource not to aphrodisiacs but to the male principle in the spirit (the animus as we should call it), and, rubbing her private parts on the stone lingam, goes back to her husband and conceives. This is because at least a certain modicum of spiritual union with the husband is necessary to supplement the biological union if pregnancy is to result. Similar results are achieved in Europe today by the psychological process of rescuing the woman's positive animus from the depths of the personal unconscious into which it has often sunk.

Our Lady similarly but on a yet deeper level worshipped and abased herself before the Lord to such an extent that her virginity, that is to say her spiritual pregnancy, blossomed also into a biological one in which spirit and matter were united in the Person of Christ. "Ever-Virgin" therefore means "Ever-Pregnant". And this Virgin Woman gave birth to the Virgin Son who himself is not only ever-pregnant through the working of the Holy Spirit, but also, in Church tradition, became her Spouse, fulfilling thus within the hearts of men not just the secondary sacred marriage with the Sister as so many pre-Christian culture-heroes do, but the primary union with the Mother who is on this spiritual level the ultimate goal.

Thus the incest taboo leads in full circle out of the biological sphere into the spiritual. This circle is well typified in the two incidents of the Gospel story as related by St. John, the first being at the outset of our Lord's career when he said to Mary, "Woman, what have I to do with thee?" (John 2, 4), and the second when on the Cross he committed her into the charge of the beloved disciple, saying "Behold thy Mother" (John 19, 27). Of these two utterances the first, spoken in connection with Christ's first miracle of turning the water into wine at the marriage in Cana, represents the taboo against union with the actual mother; whilst the second represents the consummation, of this union not in the flesh but in the spirit. The "beloved disciple", held to have been John who was also a celibate and represents therefore the mystical body, is here mystically united with the Virgin Mother who henceforth becomes the positive mother-anima-image of Christendom.

Thus Mary at Cana represents the First Eve, the externalized mother archetype who is rejected, or "sacrificed" from the point of view of external human standards, and the same Mary during the Crucifixion, who at that instant finally gives up her Son, becomes fulfilled in that she becomes "the Mother of all living" the internalized mother-archetype in a new spiritual and mystic sense.

To sum up, the point which we have now reached, the Garden of Eden represents the uncontaminated womb in which Adam and his anima, the First Eve, live in god-like communion. Then comes the Fall, when God speaks with two voices, firstly as "God" forbidding the eating of the one fruit which would make men "as gods", and secondly with the voice of the serpent telling man that he should eat it. The earthy nature of the serpent clearly corresponds to the earthy nature which Christ took on at the Incarnation when he "Who knew no sin" was "made to be sin on our behalf" (R. V. 2. Cor. 5, 21), and it will be remembered that when in the desert men grumbled and were bitten by fiery serpents the Lord commanded Moses "Make thee a fiery serpent, and set it upon a pole: and it shall come to pass, that every one that is bitten, when he looketh upon it, shall live" (Numbers 21, 8), and this brazen serpent has always been taken to be a type of Christ, the conscious Saviour who heals the complementary unconscious ill. So that the Fall came to be looked on as a felix culpa, or "fortunate sin" that dragged man out of his state of unconscious participation with the divine, causing him to pass through the vale of tears called "projection" in order finally to force him, if he is not to destroy himself, into internalizing the mother-archetype in the form of a conscious redirection of will-power towards the anima within.

Seen from this standpoint the incest taboo is not therefore just a negative prohibition, but is a positive command to seek the kingdom of heaven not in the marriage of the flesh but in the marriage within. And this is why priests have to carry the taboo to its uttermost limits and remain celibate, because it is almost if not quite impossible to achieve both kinds of marriage at once, and the ideal at least of the internal marriage has to be upheld even for the married to reach out to so far as they can[1].

Virginity as the "magic circle" of individuation.

So much from the point of view of the man. As to that of the woman, I propose first to make one short quotation from St. Bernard, and then quote the dream of a woman which first opened my eyes to the meaning of the virginity problem. St. Bernard is talking to monks, but what he says is of such universal application that it will be as good an introduction as any. In the same sermon on Conversion from which I have already quoted he says: "Thou hast sinned; cease from sinning... long has the overflowing cesspit been poisoning the whole house with its intolerable stench; vain is it for thee while still the filth flows in to pump it out, to repent while as yet thou dost not cease to sin... Shut the windows, watch the approaches,

---

[1] See Harding op. cit., p. 271, quoting Philo of Alexandria: „For the congress of men for the procreation of children makes virgins women. But when God begins to associate with the soul, he brings to pass that she who was formerly woman becomes virgin again"; also p. 275 regarding the nun's union with God.

bar the openings with care¹; and so at last, when no fresh filth comes in, thou wilt be able to purge out the old.²" Then, after proceeding along the lines already quoted, he goes on to describe the soul when it has been thus purged, saying, "It is an enclosed garden where a sealed fountain derives into four heads and from one vein of wisdom fourfold virtue flows... There the ointment of the spouse yields its most fragrant odour and the rest of sweet smells pervade when the north wind has fled and the south wind blows gently. There in the midst is the tree of life, that apple-tree of the Song of Songs, more precious than all the trees of the wood, whose shadow refreshes the spouse and whose fruit is sweet to her taste. There shines the fair beauty of continence and the vision of pure truth irradiates the heart's eyes; moreover to the ears the most sweet voice of the inward consoler brings joy and gladness³."

In the true style of the Fathers of the Church he packs into this brief passage quotations from Genesis, the Song of Songs and the Psalms, treating the whole Bible as a spiral structure in which the same themes occur almost endlessly on different levels and in varying contexts. But what interests us here is the concept of the magic circle that must be closed in order that the union with the spouse may be consummated, as also the fact that this magic circle is the same in the beginning as at the end, with the four rivers of Eden representing for us the four psychological functions, and the Tree of Life figuring, as in Apocalypse, in the New Jerusalem as well as in the Old.

This magic circle is at one and the same time the womb,

---

[1] My italics.
[2] De Conversione, p. 13.
[3] De conversione, p. 35.

the mother and the inviolate soul. The breaking of it lets
in the "filth" and the sealing of it brings salvation.

Dreams demonstrating the inner meaning of Virginity as Pregnant Womanhood (with special reference to four ancestresses of Christ).

I will now end this paper by citing the case of a very
vital woman who came into analysis because the man she
was living with had become impotent. Or rather, he came
into analysis first, but she quickly followed as soon as it
became evident that the fault was not only his but was one
arising out of their relationship and therefore coming from
both sides. Part of her trouble was that she suffered from
an extreme split in her animus-image, as a result of which
she had come to divide men into two categories. One category
was composed of "dark" fascinating intellectual men
whose talk was both inspiring to listen to and who also, as
she said, always brought out the best in her so that with
them she also shone with intellectual brilliance, but who,
for some unaccountable reason, always "let her down".
The other category comprised what she described as "fair"
men, who were slow, lacking in fire, dull, listless, stupid
and not at all successful by wordly standards – indeed not
by any standards at all, since they had neither push nor
determination to get on in life, and no real sexual attraction.
Yet it was to one of the latter category to whom,
after having been "let down" by a "dark" man, she had
fled, and had lived with for the two years preceding the
analysis while at the same time constantly complaining at
his faithful dullness.

Her first act before coming into analysis was to try

"scribbling", and what she felt to be the most meaningful of her scribblings was an impulsively drawn circle about 3 inches in diameter which was incomplete at the bottom left-hand corner, towards which breech, on the outside, she depicted, as if crawling, a small lithe snake-like form. This was quite evidently the point at which her psyche "leaked", both letting out what should be internalised psychic contents and at the same time admitting on the rebound the evil influence, the snake obviously being the sign of intellectual contamination (a mixture of fear and pride) which was ever on the look-out to destroy the virgin integrity of her soul. This incomplete circle threatened by the snake, occupying the right hand or conscious part of her sheet of paper, corresponded with the exciting desires towards the "dark" man. But this configuration was balanced by the presence, on the left upper side of the paper, of a kind of sluggish dragon-like creature of quite uncertain sex, depicting equally clearly the (to her) dull and uneventful union with the "fair" man which she at present had, but from which nevertheless she was unable to extricate herself precisely because the motivation for it was, to her, unconscious, and the only reason she could vocally give for continuing it was because, as she said, it was at least "safe".

The safety was, of course, one of stagnation, just as the danger of the other was the extremity of passion.

The problem was how to transform both these negative unions in the unconscious by uniting them into a single positive union in the conscious. For both conditions depicted in the "scribbling" were conditions of extreme participation mystique, that with her present partner who belonged to the "dull, fair" type, being manifestly inactive in the conscious though intensely active in the unconscious, whereas her previous connection with the "exciting, dark" man was active in her conscious life, but, as the event had proved, inactive or only negatively active in the unconcious.

That is to say that both types of union failed because of the "leakage", on the one hand a leakage of psychic contents into the external world causing, as Jung puts it, a "primitive identity of the ego with ourselves, in other words, a complete absence of relationship"[1] and a wholesale projection; and on the other hand that internal contamination of the viriginal psyche due to the introjection into it of false notions which is the antecedent cause of all such external projections. In other words, in her case, though Adam and Eve had been ejected from the Garden of Eden, the Angel with the flaming sword had not taken up his place at the entrance, so that what should be divided (in the conscious, i. e. differentiated) was not, and what should not be divided (in the unconscions) was. In yet other words, with her the spiritual incest taboo had not come into operation, and, like Lot's wife, in turning back towards the city of contamination (i. e. mother-fixation, which in the biblical story took the form of active homosexuality), her heart had indeed become turned to stone. For the one legitimate relationship of participation mystique is that existing between mother and child within the womb, corresponding to Adam and Eve within the Garden, and to purely biological mating before the incest taboo. All looking back is ultimately a search to re-establish this blissful union in the flesh, and all looking forward is the effort to establish it in the spirit.

[1] C. G. Jung, Contributions to Analytical Psychology, London 1928, p. 190.

What in the analysis transpired was that in remaining tied in a condition of participation mystique with the "dull, fair" man, the dreamer was, in fact, seeking to re-capture the infantile incestuous relationship with her father, and that he was in her similarly seeking to recapture his mother. And in both cases, as evidenced by the duration of their union, this unconscious consideration quite overrode the adult sexual mating instinct and had, in fact, nullified it by rendering him impotent, till such a time as the various factors in the situation could be sorted out.

As a matter of fact they later married and reared a family.

The line taken by the analyst was "If this apparently dull, unsatisfying and on the surface negative union has gone on for so long, there must be something positive in it to keep it going at all". This led to a simultaneous analysis of both partners, each of whom after a certain stage started dreaming about prostitutes, he dreaming that he was searching for one, and she that she was herself becoming one.

The prostitute is the archetype of the free woman, the woman untrammelled by man's laws. For dreams are on this level the complementary opposite of life in the flesh. In external life she has to pay a price much heavier than that paid by the man, but in dreams she represents the bountiful earth-mother[1], uncontaminated by thinking, who offers good things to all men and who is to be had for the

---

[1] See Harding, op. cit., p. 78, on the subject of Ishtar being referred to as „The Prostitute", and of the Chinese Holy Virgin who bore a son while yet a virgin and is patroness of prostitutes; also p. 94, on which she quotes from a Roman Catholic book on the Saints the legend of how Mary the Gipsy or the Egyptian, whose face was black, „wishing to go to the Holy Land on a pilgrimage was to offer herself as a prostitute to the sailors on a vessel bound for that shore".

asking, though the asking involves toiling with the sweat of one's brow, to dig, harrow, manure, and plant the soil. She is, in fact, the ultimate anima, the temple priestess who marries the god and bestows her favours upon devout men[1], thus raising them also to semi-divine status. On this spiritual level she is also Our Lady, who showers her gifts freely upon all men and who is profligate (note the word) with her divine favours. In fact she is in the psyche the Virgin Unspotted, pregnant with the boundless pregnancy of nature, translated into this spiritual sphere.

Why else should it be that not only was Our Lord's mother both unmarried and called Virgin, but that every one of the other four women mentioned in Christ's genealogy[2] as given in the first chapter of St. Matthew should be of a character that the modern, and indeed also the ancient, conventional outlook would label as "immoral"? These four, selected not haphazard but evidently with deliberate intent and leaving out all the respectably married ancestresses like Sarah, were: –

a) Tamar, who, disguising herself as a common prostitute, seduced her father-in-law Judah.

b) Rahab, the most prominent professional harlot in the

---

[1] See Harding, op. cit., pp. 268–70 regarding the hieros gamos, saying that „for the woman the significance of the experience must have been in her submission to instinct".

[2] This is, of course, the genealogy of Christ as traced through Joseph, which would appear to deny Virgin Birth. Luke (Chapter 3) has a much longer one leading back to Adam, who is there called „the son of God". The Matthew genealogy goes back only to David, and is designed to show Christ's royal lineage. Both gospelwriters notice the discrepancy regarding the Virgin Birth, Matthew by simply referring to Joseph as „the husband of Mary", and Luke by saying that Christ was Joseph's son „as was supposed". The inference is either that, if Joseph was not in fact his father, Mary was also of the same lineage and that the two might be first cousins (as were Mary and Elizabeth), in which case their marriage would be in line with that of Jacob and Rachel; or else simply that Christ, being adopted by Joseph, would in law be reckoned to be his son. In either case the genealogy, placed thus in the forefront of the New Testament, cannot be due to chance but must be of deep psychological import.

Old Testament, who, however, repented and is held up as a model of repentance in the Epistles.

c) Ruth, who seduced her husband's kinsman Boaz.

d) Bath-sheba, "her that had been the wife of Urias", whom David abducted and whose husband he treacherously caused to be killed in battle but who nevertheless became the mother of Solomon.

St. Jerome, in his Commentary on Matthew, says: – This was so designed in order that He who had come for the sake of sinners might, being born of sinners, blot out the sins of all, because He came not now as a Judge, but as a Physician, to heal our diseases". This explanation, as those also put forward by St. Chrysostom and others, may be true on one level, but from the point of view from which this paper is written the reason for the inclusion of these four women alone in this genealogy, is that they are all "virgins" in the sense that they represent undifferentiated womanhood, contaminated indeed on the conscious level of man's laws (though in the Bible story these matters are later accomodated), but uncontaminated in the spiritual virginity or integrity which prompted their actions. Nor were they (with the exception of Rahab, whose motherhood is recorded only in the Matthew genealogy and the circumstances of which therefore we do not know) just repentant sinners who later made respectable marriages, but it was actually out of their "immoral" unions that the ancestral line of Christ as traced through Joseph arose.

A whole paper could be devoted to an analysis of the stories of these four women, and of their roles as representing respectively the four psychological functions of womanhood as symbolised by the four rivers of Eden of which Mary is the head. I have the manuscript of such a paper already written, but it cannot be included here, and I must now return to the dreams of the modern woman already mentioned, an understanding of which throws much light on the whole problem of spiritual virginity as symbolised in dreams by sexual freedom, dreams being, it must always be remembered, on this deep level the very opposite of external life.

I propose to discuss only two dreams, both dreamt at a critical period of the analysis, in the first of which the dreamer found herself going down into a large underground room like a restaurant, which she at first took to be a night club but later realised was a brothel with women sitting at tables and sailors coming in and out. First mildly interested at this, she suddenly became horrified when the duenna of the place flung her arms round her and gave her a smacking kiss, and said "Dearie, you are one of us. You will never get away from here now." The horror was in the dream. When she woke up, being already partially analysed, she began to overcome her horror and look more objectively at the situation. "Underground" meant, of course, the unconscious, where things are apt to be the reverse of what they seem. A prostitute is, from the male point of view, a totally undifferentiated woman, just Woman, who will give him what he wants on this undifferentiated level. Since differentiation is a thing that belongs to the conscious which is symbolised by "above-ground", this undifferentiation in the unconscious means for a woman freedom from the trammels of ego-consciousness and therefore the discovery of her true self. Apart from personal associations which so often distort archetypal patterns – and there were none in this dream – sailors and airmen always represent Spirit, though each represents spirit of a different kind, like the waters above and below the firmament. Airmen represent the volatile, male "Holy Ghost" aspect of spirit, and sailors its ponderable, heavy or earthy aspect, which is just what this woman needed to counteract her over-intellectualised flights that often carried her quite beyond the bounds set by the reality of a situation, and that made real and lasting contacts with actual men impossible or at least extremely difficult.

There were, of course, far too many sailors in the dream, allowing much too much choice and freedom to escape from any one of them. But, for the stage she was at, the dream was a very positive one, and the duenna's greeting and statement that she would "never get away from here now" meant that the analytical process had well bitten in, and that she could no longer escape from really facing up to her problems; that, in fact, the ground for salvation was already there. The duenna indeed represented the positive earthmother.

The next dream is the really vital one for the thesis of this paper. She dreamt that she was to be a blood-donor, and for this purpose had gone into a large hall, at the end of which was a table at which stood or sat a lady doctor. The room was full of other prospective blood-donors, all of whom were friends whom the dreamer had known in external life. The lady doctor was one whom she had previously known also in real life, and whom she had not very much liked. What was her horror therefore when this lady doctor asked her in a loud voice so that all could hear: "Are you a virgin?" and went on "Because if you are not a virgin, you won't do. Your hole will be too big." The dreamer thought it, to say the least, a bit tactless on the part of the lady doctor to say this so loud, though in fact all her friends in the room knew all about her. So she had to admit that she was not. So far, the scene was at least comprehensible, but what was her amazement when the lady doctor added "But these two will do. They are virgins", and pointed to two girls the dreamer had known in her youth, both of whom she had envied on account of the extreme ease of their relationship with men, whereas she herself had suffered from great inhibitions, and both of whom were now married and had children. Yet they were dubbed virgins and pronounced good as blood-donors, and she was not. With this puzzle in her mind she woke up.

The first question put to her was what the lady doctor had meant by saying that her hole would be too big, and what this could have with blood-doning. The latter part of the question she was unable to answer, but she said that the first part immediately called to her mind a picture of the "dark" lover's member penetrating her. This concept called vividly to mind her original "scribbling" of the incomplete circle threatened by the lithe snakelike object, and it immediately became clear what in this dream "virginity" meant. That it did not refer to physical virginity was clear from the fact that though none of the three were physically virgins, the two successfully married women, both of whom had produced children, were regarded as being "virgins", whereas she herself was not. What the dream did mean was, on the contrary, that whereas with the two married women thinking had not contaminated feeling, that is to say that "moral" values quite proper in themselves and if confined to consciousness, had in their case not got loose from their proper sphere and penetrated into the unconscious where they become the reverse. In other words, these two women had not contaminated their fundamental womanhood and had maintained ease of relations both with their own souls and with men, and were therefore spiritually "pregnant virgins"; whereas the dreamer herself, through faulty upbringing and the psychological muddle in which her parents had lived, had "moral" values shoved down her throat too early and therefore had contaminated her soul by substituting thinking for feeling, and thus could not establish proper relations either with her soul or with men. And so the paradox comes about that the married mothers with children were spiritual virgins, but that she herself was not. The virginity of the dream has nothing to do with physical virginity but everything to do with that of the soul[1]. Virginity of the soul means uncontamination and therefore pregnancy of the soul leading to easy pregnancy of the body. But lack of virginity of the soul means lack of pregnancy both in soul and sometimes also in body, because lack of pregnancy (which means lack of spiritual "virginity") in the soul prevents satisfactory relationship with any man, and in her case had reacted upon the man she was now living with in such a way as to make him impotent too, though it could not have done so had he not had asimilar contamination of feeling by thinking in his psychological make-up also.

This dream, of course, raises many other questions which there is no space to go into here. So I will confine myself to saying that the symbol of the "unclosed hole" occurs in a sexual context not only in women's dreams but also in men's. A man of thirty, suffering from extreme retarded development due to an over-masculine mother and over-

---

[1] This is what Esther Harding means by her constant references to a woman being "one-in-herself" (op. cit., p. 80 and elsewhere).

feminine father, dreamt constantly that he penetrated his mother or mother-substitute and that when he withdrew the "hole" remained open. This meant that the magic circle of his inner integrity had never closed, that is to say that, though physically a virgin, his spiritual virginity had never been sufficiently established, and that he was ceaselessly open to the influence of the false thinking mechanisms of his mother, whom he at once hated but from whom at the same time he could never get really free. In other words, the psychological incest taboo had never been established with him either.

With this I must bring this overlong essay to a close, apologising both to Professor Jung and to the reader for the fact that, owing to war-time conditions, it has not proved possible to condense or work over it as closely as might otherwise have been the case.

It has been my object in it to establish the two-fold purpose of the incest taboo by first demonstrating its manifest content which is the expansion of society, and then indicating its complementary opposite latent content which is the fulfilment within the psyche of that which the taboo forbids us so stringently in the flesh, namely the union with the uncontaminated mother-principle represented by the spiritual return into the womb. The words of the Salve Regina addressed to the Virgin Mother, "and after this our exile, show us the blessed fruit of thy womb Jesus" describe the process better than any. For on this level the incest taboo is the exile, which cuts mankind off from the object of his most intense desire in order that, through exile from it in the flesh, he may rediscover it in the spirit, and, having re-entered the womb, be born again.

ON PSYCHIC CONSCIOUSNESS

By JOHN LAYARD

CONTENTS AND SUMMARY

Page

I. Introduction 277
  On the meaning of psychic consciousness. A Malekulan example 277
  The Incest Taboo creating the "two laws". Hermaphroditic Perception 281
  Triadic Formulae. The Third Factor 284
  Society as the Male Mother in contrast to the Female Father. Superego contrasted with Psychic Consciousness 287
  The "doubling" of the personality. Further fragmentation, leading to increasing complexity of character, simplified by the uniting function of psychic consciousness. The slaying of the God 290

II. Biblical 292
  Nebuchadnezzar and Daniel. Internalising the External Image 292
  Analytical Parallel. Daniel as Psychotherapist 295
  "Thou art this head of gold." The four "kingdoms" 297
  "Bruising." The Iron and the Clay. The psychic "seed of man" 298
  "Judgment" 299
  The four-fold Tables of the Law (the "stone" uniting them), and the Four-section Kinship System 301
  The Stone "cut out without hands". The Iron and Clay "mingle" but do not "cleave". Incest Taboo and Sacrifice 302
  The "doubling" of Nebuchadnezzar and of Job through the addition of psychic consciousness based on the father-principle 304
  The necessary destruction 306

III. Malekulan 307
  Transition. The primitive meaning of "stone". Earth symbolising the Soul 307
  Stone and Tusked Boar. The Sister-Anima 310
  The Spirit and the Withholding Soul. Psychic life here and now ... 311
  Sister-exchange and the four-section kinship system. The All-Father and the lack of recognised ancestors 312
  Disruption of the sister-exchanging system in favour of an open one giving more scope to individuality 316
  Homo-erotic consequence. Relationship with the bride's brother the basis of initiation and impregnation by the spirits of the ancestors 317
  Society as the "possessive mother" or externalised "withholding soul" relaxes her grip. Newcomers challenge mothers' brothers and found patrilineages 319
  The female "flesh and blood" and the male "bone" 321
  A third element intrudes. Bride-price in tusked boars replaces the sister given in exchange. The boar a symbol for incest. Three brothers-in-law replace two, leading to the foundation of three patrilineages 321
  Comparative free choice. Detachment, "not cleaving". Closed kinship system becomes an "open" one. Five patrilineages and the Pentacle. Five patri-villages. Odd and even numbers 324

E-rets and Le-rets. The Culture-hero with his sister-wife. The Logos called "The Word"	328
The "two laws". E-rets "doubled" in personality and his whole village doubled in size. The sister-spouse in the Song of Solomon. Krishna, Portia "another Daniel". Nebuchadnezzar and Job	331
IV. Conclusions	334
The Clay and the Stone. Weakness and strength of Love	334
Stone and the initiating Great Mother with Ten "Sons". The God of Light marries their Sister, thus giving rise to a collective Sister-Anima. A hundred tusked boars given in exchange	335
The "inner light" transforms incest. Stone and the spirits of the ancestors	338
Destruction precedes rebirth. The withholding soul yields her treasure up	341

I.

INTRODUCTION

On the meaning of psychic consciousness
A Malekulan example

Si jeunesse savait, si vieillesse pouvait, "if the young knew, and the old could but do", may be interpreted as a sigh of old-age regret, or may be taken otherwise as a sign that there are things which the old can do which the young cannot do. For in the symbolism of masculinity there are the two opposite poles of the *puer aeternus* and "the wise old man". These are symbols not only of youth and age but of two modes of experience which we may describe as nature and psyche which interpenetrate, each having its own sphere but being the poorer without the other one.

Each symbolises a dynamic process revolving in opposite directions around potential consciousness which grows in proportion as they are united, and the old can at the same time be young, while the young bring with them the archetypal wisdom of the past which is old enough. But the old can be yet younger than the young in realising consciously what youth experiences as a rule only unconsciously.

This second consciousness of the psychic creative process, which youth has but does not know, is what is sometimes called "the unconscious", or "the creative unconscious", but I here propose to call it by the more dynamic term *psychic consciousness,* as opposed to ego-consciousness, indicating its hidden nature, developing a will of its own in the womb of time which will transform the will of man's first nature and ultimately transcend it. It is this will, born of nature but at the same time *out* of it, as a man-child issues out of the mother's womb, which a man may be lucky if he can make contact with, and submit his ego to it and to its rich experience. As the child unwitting of the world learns to submit to it and learn from it, so in the second half of life the externals drop off, and the old may learn submission to the internal life of the child re-born.

Without consciousness of this inner womb which gives birth to psychic life, old age may wither in unhappiness and a sense of frustration. With it, the personality may expand internally as it decays externally. Internal is psychic, and thus unseen. It is the stuff of immortality supposed to survive after death in what is often called the "afterlife". But it is an afterlife that begins in this life and is, from this point of view, its "child", the *puer aeternus* coming to fruition in the old wise man, whose body and emotions are the matrix in which it incubates and grows. Nature thus incubates the psyche which will survive when nature dies.

Such concepts are universal, and are obscured only from time to time when, in some highly developed civilisations, a fake spirituality so overwhelms them that, with the contempt of nature, the psyche which is nature's child is apt to perish too.

Primitive man does not suffer so much from such misconceptions as we do, since he is closer to nature, and thus to all those psychic forces operating behind nature. His rituals and mythological beliefs revolve around the concept of the afterlife which at the same time is here and now in embryo, and as a foetus develops by means of sacrifice both ritual and internal. Life and the afterlife go hand in hand.

Thus, in Malekula, an old man ripe in years, formed inwardly through much transforming sacrifice of which the external symbol is the sacrifice of tusked boars, but the internal meaning is the sacrifice of incest which psychologically is self-regard, will often carry out his own mortuary rites while he is yet alive. The superficial or external view of this is that he wants to make sure that all the proper rituals will be performed, designed to please the ancestors and to placate the Female Ghost or goddess whose grand desire it is to destroy men's spirits and thus to prevent immortality. But she is in fact an initiating goddess, demanding inwardly the very sacrifice that outwardly she jealously tries to prevent, according to the myth which describes her as a devourer who, if her secret purpose is understood, confers immortal life, said to be lived in the centre of an active volcano on a neighbouring island, whose fire is "her fire", a fire which, if accepted, does not burn but maintains psychic life in perpetuity[1].

Thus the real meaning is that the old man in this way signifies that he is already "dead" and reborn as a child (he actually may not feed himself but must be fed) and that he has thus already joined the spirits of the ancestors who are themselves reborn. By doing this he claims to have himself at least partly "become spirit" and is thus one with all those who previously have gone before him in the acquirement of second childhood or psychic power, called by various forms of the word *mana*, which makes them immortal. This power is recognised by his contemporaries, both young and old, and he is called *ta-mats*, which means "dead man", a term here used not in abuse or disregard but with a feeling of awe, since he is now known to have acquired at least a measure of immortality during life and thus become "doubled". He now has a body, not only of aging flesh and blood, but in addition, replacing the youthful vigour which he has lost, a second psychic body "doubling" the first one, for which he is revered and feared. For he is now recognised as being not only "child" but that child's mother too, having acquired female receptive attributes as well as male, thus giving him the right to adopt the title of "Lord Mother" or "Mother of the Place" or "Mother of the People" as I have described elsewhere[2].

Having become once more a small "man-child", he now exerts authority by virtue of the Great Mother whose child he is, mother and child

---

[1] 1938, pp. 253 ff.; 1942, pp. 218 ff.; 1956, pp. 378 ff.
[2] 1955, p. 24; 1956, p. 383.

being here one, as they are in infancy; though here the two roles are reversed, for the "mother", formerly external, is now internalised, the male acting now as her interpreter and executive, no longer dependent on her, but as equal partners. He has thus become psychically hermaphrodite, having through sacrifice regained that unity with the female principle which a small infant has with its human mother, whom a boy abandons at initiation at the hands of men, but as an adult recaptures archetypally through union with the Female Ghost, or "anima within", thus giving birth to the spirit.

This spirit is what may be thought of as that "inner masculinity", born of the pregnant anima, which in this paper I call "psychic consciousness".

The process of development of psychic consciousness out of the matrix of the female or collective, or instinctive unconscious, though varying in detail, is basically the same throughout the world, in all ages and climes, and the purpose of this lecture is to enquire by means of illustrations into the kind of way in which it emerges into fuller consciousness.

We are today so complex, so identified with our own personal emotions, and so carried along by the society in which we live, that a historical perspective may help us to observe ourselves, and to see in facts recorded for us from the past, or else observed by anthropologists with regard to primitive kinship and mythology, something of what this process is that we are part of, but are so intimately part of that it is sometimes difficult for us to understand, failing some such broader view.

The founders of modern psychology invented the non-committal term "unconscious" to indicate that there are factors which the average man with a workaday ego-consciousness sufficient to his everyday needs does not understand, and as a rule ignores. The time is past, however, in which we can be just content with non-committal terms when, in point of fact, we are beginning to know something about this so-called "unconscious" as it is revealed to us in mythology and dreams, and in those mystical experiences which the mystics find so difficult to describe but do their best to communicate to us. It is a fact, of course, that we cannot understand their writings unless we have paid sufficient attention to ourselves to have had some faintly similar experience, which we may compare with theirs and thus widen our horizon, or rather "deepen" it, finding inside ourselves an immanence which corresponds with what they may describe either as immanent (happening within) or as transcendant, conceived of as coming from without.

For the psychologist the "within" and the "without" are in this sense the same, since the perception occurs in any case "within". The contrast is not thus so much between the immanent and the transcendant or, in terms of everyday life, the individual and society, as between what ego knows of both or does not know, namely that "other", which clearly has a will of its own quite independently of ego-consciousness and often apparently opposed to it.

The Incest Taboo creating the "two laws"
Hermaphroditic Perception

I do not wish here to complicate matters by going into the presumed details of psychological structure, other than to call attention to the initial contrast between ego-consciousness and psychic consciousness, and the potential relationship between them which may be most conducive to full life. For present purposes we may regard ego-consciousness as being that part of the personality, including the persona, which has been formed largely by society, as mediated through the environment, which, through imitation, the individual identifies himself with to a greater or less extent, depending as time passes on how successfully he fits in with it, or fails to fit in with it. Whatever else a man may have in him of complex reactions may be regarded as being prompted by psychic consciousness, a term which covers both instinct and the reactions of instinct to the frustrations imposed by society, which may be positive or negative, creative or uncreative, according to the measure of his perception of what these frustrations really aim at with regard to the transformation of childhood emotions into adult ones, in the inner instead of on the outer plane.

The prime mover in life causing the split between the two is the incest taboo on which all human society is founded, which we in the West have so ingrained in us that we hardly think about it, but which gives rise to problems so conscious to all primitive peoples that their whole life revolves around the question of how to transform incest into a *hieros gamos* within, which is incest internalised, transmuted into its opposite as the matrix of psychic consciousness.

The result of this taboo is the formation of the two main opposing forces which together constitute the formative factor in all primitive civilisations:—

(a) the organisation of kinship so as to prevent incest in the flesh, while providing the necessary outlet in the marriage between near relatives which, though nearly incestuous, is not actually so;

(b) the growth of mythology in the complementary opposite direction, leaving men's fancy free to roam in the attempt to satisfy internally all those desires which are forbidden in the flesh and which, if thus transformed, go to build up the soul or anima which is the mother of spirit or psychic consciousness.

It is this split which is the subject of all creation myths, all of which deal with the creation, not of the world of matter, but of the psyche to be created out of matter or primary natural desires. While on the speculative religious level, the contrast may appear as that between transcendance and immanence, on the social level the workings of the split may be more clearly seen in the opposition between society and the individual, which can be creative or destructive depending on society's and the individual's understanding of it.

As a basic problem of existence, there thus appear at first sight to be not one law but "two laws" which are opposed, the law externally expressed in the strict regulations of society, and the law internally expressed in the often quite contrary movements of the heart or the imaginative faculties.

A classic formulation of such contrast is that of the twin concepts in Jewish thinking of on the one hand *Halakah*, meaning "the Law", the law of social and ritualised behaviour laid down to be observed explicitly, and on the other hand what is called *Aggadah*, which Scholem translates as "Legend"[3] and includes myth with all its numerous possibilities of interpretation, as well as what psychologists would call "active imagination" and is the stuff of dreams.

Aggadah, with its untrammelled freedom of imagination and free association of both thought and images, has at times been thought so antithetical to the Law that some have wished to suppress it, while others have despaired at making any synthesis. But from the psychological angle both are indispensable as the two poles of life, *Halakah* (the Law) being equated with what we here call ego-consciousness in its collective social form, and *Aggadah* with the dynamic inner life without which all the law in the world would be quite empty of meaning and indeed destructive.

There are in this way what we might think of as "two laws". On the one hand, the law of outward observance, finite, rigid and codified. On the other hand, the law of inner movement, fluid, uncodified, uncodifiable and infinite. It is to man's perception of this law that, if I understand him right, Scholem refers when he speaks of "mystical consciousness" (p. 9), "mythical consciousness" (p. 22), and in another place "religious consciousness" (p. 24). It is what I call psychic consciousness, a term which may be used to cover all those wells of inner perception that may or may not seep through to, and be accepted by, ego-consciousness, however unwilling the latter may so often be to honour them, or even to admit their existence.

What heals the breach is the realisation of the third thing which can reconcile both. This thing is from one angle "sacrifice", that which reveals the opposite in everything, creating a central ego strengthened to face both opposites and to combine them in a single act of submission based on the ability to "think double". This is a mode of thought leading to the knowledge that there is no good which does not contain some evil, and no evil that may not contain the germ of good. In it what appears male may at any moment become female, and female become male, in

---

[3] GERSHOM G. SCHOLEM, *Major Trends in Jewish Mysticism*, London, Thames and Hudson, 1955, p. 28.

such a way as to produce that kind of hermaphroditic perception that is attributed always to divinity, and that man also may reflect if he can hold himself open to receive both impacts without resisting them.

This is the third factor which "sees" both inner and outer, the world of men and the world of archetypes which operate inside those men, expressed always in the trinitarian imagery of the two united in the one. The medium of transformation is inevitably the middle one, which for a man appears female, and for a woman appears male. For a man it is the anima or feminine perception which, standing between the two, both ego-consciousness and psychic consciousness, alone can unite them, since, being always ambivalent, this anima, like the Female Ghost of Malekulan mythology, can face both ways, and, if impregnated by due attention being paid to her, can give birth to that "inner masculinity", or psychic consciousness, which is the result of such union.

Triadic Formulae. The Third Factor

There are two images for this process in world religions. There is the Christian image that Christ as Creator created his own Virgin Mother in order to give birth to him as the "inner man" indwelling in humanity, a function later taken over by the Holy Ghost. The Virgin Mother is thus daughter and mother in one, and is as such dual. She is "virgin" because she is "one in herself" and cannot be seduced. She is "mother" because she gives herself to the spirit which she both receives and bears, in her humility and her humanity. She is the same "before, during and after" psychic conception and the giving birth, which are potentially continuous, for she is "always there".

Christ is thus at one and the same time the Creator, as an aspect of "the old wise man", or Father-figure, who knows how to honour and impregnate his daughter with his own psychic substance, and as her Son he is the *puer aeternus*, the inner aspect of the old wise man, born of his honouring her.

The Moslem image, on the contrary, is that the Prophet's daughter Fatima gave birth to *him* so that he might beget *her*. Thus said to have been her own father's mother, this is an image of a woman conscious of her animus, and of a man, the Prophet, conscious of the two aspects of his feminity, symbolised by the mother who gives birth and the daughter who is begotten of this union of mother and of son. The spirit here is feminine, as in Christianity it is masculine.

If we contrast the two we get Figure 1.

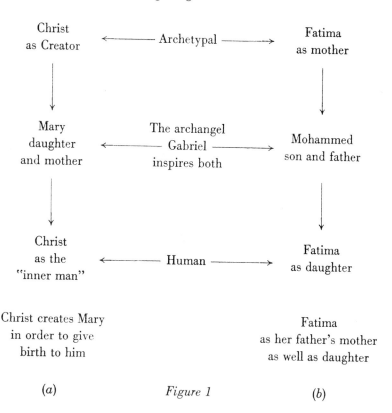

Figure 1

But if we realise that Mohammed arose 500 years later than Christ, also in desert land, and combine the two as a historically evolving process, we get Figure 2:—

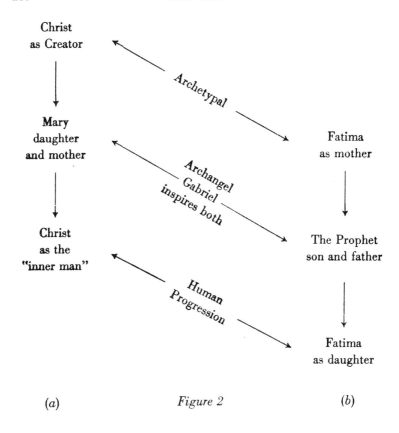

Figure 2

in which Fatima may be seen as another later aspect of Mary, the Prophet as another aspect of the spirit of prophecy acknowledging the Christ as forerunner, and, the developing series being one of alternating contrasexuality, or animus and anima alternately begetting or giving birth to their opposites in continuous exchange.

Christ as Creator of his mother and Fatima giving birth to her own father Mohammed are both archetypical concepts having to do with pure spirit, whereas the human Mary and the human Christ, the human Prophet and his daughter Fatima belong to humanity inspired with spirit which, lacking humanity, is without form, as mankind would also be without form lacking spirit.

It is therefore significant that the link between spirit and matter is in both cases the archangel Gabriel, who in Christian tradition awoke in Mary the awareness of her inspired condition, and in Moslem tradition inspired Mohammed with the words, uttered in trance-state, which later were collected and became the Koran, which for the Mohammedans is the inspired Word. What is in Christian belief the Word becoming flesh corresponds in Mohammedan belief to the Word uttered by Mohammed when thus inspired, though not when speaking as an ordinary man. Both images refer to psychic consciousness (in contrast to ego-consciousness) mediated by the feminine element in man, or the male element in woman. "The Word became flesh" indicates the unity of ego-consciousness with psychic consciousness.

The Word may be symbolically male or female, as the contrasexual element giving rise to, and in turn issuing from a human being of opposite bodily sex, as the father-principle in a woman giving rise to the spirit "son", or the mother-principle in a man giving rise to the spirit "daughter". The three in union create the whole man or woman as the case may be. The three is also four, in that the middle function in each case faces both ways, being in the first case both daughter and mother, and in the second case, son and father.

Society as the Male Mother in contrast to the Female Father
Superego contrasted with Psychic Consciousness

In human life as we see it and move in it, what is transcendant is Society as the Male Mother of us all, in whom we "live and move and have our being" on this earth, and serve or grumble at.

For though society is organised by men, it is collectively female, as we know well from all our languages, which speak of a university as *alma mater,* a city as a *metro-polis,* of "Mother Church" although it is organised exclusively by men. Most peoples speak of "mother-land", as we in Britain do by calling it Britannia, though some in militaristic sense may, like the Germans, call it "father-land", and sometimes bring disaster on themselves for doing so. Even the French, for instance, speak of *la Patrie*, not "*le*" *Patrie*, thus indicating its motherhood even while asserting its fatherhood. Society is thus a "mother" in male form, who rears her sons, protects and brings them up, but later has to relinquish a too great possessiveness, so that the "son" may live and not be too identified with her.

The "son" thus symbolises the individual, nurtured in society as by a mother who brings him up, and which conditions him. But, in the conflict thus engendered between society and the individual, the individual who is part of it must not at the same time be so identified with it as to lose his individuality. The problem is how far society itself will become the god or goddess swamping the individual, or how far the ultimate spirit in man symbolised by the "son" can integrate itself, that is, be born out of the social matrix as out of this soul externalised. For in the main, as I have shown elsewhere[4], society and the soul are mirror opposites. Society is symbolically for a man a mother, sister and daughter in the three main phases of man's life as he grows in stature. The ultimate question is which of the two shall win, society possessing the individual, who thus may lose or never gain his individuality, or the individual using society for the incubation of his own spirit which will outlive society as it will outlive his own body.

Will psychic consciousness, that inner life, survive the pressure of society? Can it make peace with it, or will it not be born? Is ego-consciousness, identified with society, or psychic consciousness to be the good that saves? Sometimes we make the great error of identifying with it. Such are "the pillars of society", who may well support it but in doing so become blind, indentifying themselves with their own social persona and thus becoming so one-sided as to repress individuality and all those unseen factors striving for recognition, which have in them the seeds of future change and possible deeper understanding. In such a case the individual corresponds to psychic consciousness as opposed to

---

[4] See page 307; also p. 319.

society which is based on collective superego-consciousness, which we here for short call simply ego-consciousness.

The same pattern exists in each person, with the potential mediating function as anima or animus, that which can see both ways and can attempt to unify them. This may be briefly expressed in the following diagram:—

Superego
(called ego-consciousness for short)

Transcendant in two senses,
functioning outwardly as Society as the great

Male-Mother,

inwardly as identification with Society

●

| The mediating two-sided Anima or Animus |

●

Psychic Consciousness

The Individual
The Spirit immanent in Man
as a man's "inner masculinity"
or a woman's "inner femininity"
born from relationship with the

Female-Father

Figure 3

The contrast to the male-mother principle of society and the social persona, which as both extravert and introjected is one regulating behaviour according to an environmentally laid-down pattern, is the opposite principle of the female-father, which means the inwardly pregnant father-principle. For as the father in matriarchal society was comparatively ignored in the mother's ego-consciousness, other than as the mere physical *progenitor,* so psychic consciousness depends on the recognition of the father as *pater* replacing the mother's brother or mother's animus as the ultimate prime mover, and the father-principle as the goal leading to rebirth into the psychic world, figuratively described in the Bible as "Abraham's bosom" (Luke 16.22) or "the bosom of the Father" (John 1.18).

The "doubling" of the personality
Further fragmentation, leading to increasing complexity of character,
simplified by the uniting function of psychic consciousness
The slaying of the god

Matriarchal dominance, from which all things visibly arise, can be pierced only as a woman can by being divided by the phallic principle thrusting up from below (within). This is equivalent to the incest taboo causing the basic split, which in the end fertilises through the breach thus made. It is equivalent also to psychic consciousness invading ego-consciousness strongly enough to persuade ego-consciousness to submit to this hidden influence, so as bring about a willing union in which the powers have changed places, psychic consciousness now dictating, with ego-consciousness acting as its executive, as second in command internally while being first in command externally.

This brings about a doubling rather than a deprivation, but only as a result of ego-consciousness splitting and splitting again many more times until, like ploughed soil that is fragmented and therefore ever more receptive to the seed of psychic consciousness, becoming ever more complex and at the same time flexible and intelligent.

This is the sacrifice that ego is called upon to make, to forces greater than itself which will eventually break it if it does not yield. To be broken, not to resist the fragmentation that divides but to accept it willingly, although at first with pain as a parturating woman does, is to receive more, not less, including the power of reflection between the parts thus divided, which may thus hold converse with one another as they cannot do while still incestuously "one", which is equivalent to remaining unconscious. It is the sacrifice of original one-ness, the mother-and-child one-ness of nature, or the society-and-me one-ness of nurture, which opens up the way to the new one-ness in duality and multiplicity which psychic consciousness promotes.

The middle and mediating factor between ego-consciousness and psychic consciousness is the third factor symbolised in Figures 1 and 2 of a human being of either sex able to receive the messages of psychic consciousness and to "utter" them either as a divine child or as words able to move multitudes. Figure 3 presents the facts more psychologically stated, in terms of the overall concept of all three main parts of the personality being hermaphroditically doubled, so as to produce an atmosphere of loving communication between them all, so that they can all be united in a "seventh" which links them all, corresponding to the third which links the two:—

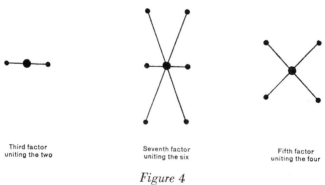

Third factor uniting the two   Seventh factor uniting the six   Fifth factor uniting the four

Figure 4

The six- or seven-fold structure is rather more, however, than most humans can bear. There must be some simplification if the individual is to survive, and psychic consciousness flourish without being too top-heavy, burdened with a social persona which it cannot support. If it is to survive, the superstructure has to go. The god has to be slain. The six must be reduced to four, the seven-fold personality to a five-fold one, on a human rather than a divine level. This is a principle so universal that it applies to idols such as identification with Society as much as it does to identification with divinity, since in the end all must be inwardised. With the crucifixion of the outer man, that is to say its death and consequent resurrection internally, the inward man becomes doubled.

This applies also to the "ideal figure" in dreams, the image of a possessive superego dominance, symbolising that function of self-regard which, if identified with, leads to the disaster of an inflation which must inevitably collapse. The question is, whether the collapse be willing or unwilling.

II.

BIBLICAL

Nebuchadnezzar and Daniel
Internalising the External Image

As first example of the universality of this problem, later to be parallelled by a Malekulan one, we may take Daniel's analysis of Nebuchadnezzar's first recorded dream, which you may remember as having been so terrible and so unacceptable to his waking self that, though he knew he had dreamt it, he could not bring himself even to remember what it was.

For "Nebuchadnezzar dreamed dreams, wherewith his spirit was troubled, and his sleep brake from him", and in distress he said, "The thing is gone from me" and threatened the astrologers and the Chaldeans "if ye will not make known unto me the dream, with the interpretation thereof, ye shall be cut in pieces, and your houses shall be made a dunghill". But none were found, and they protested "There is not a man upon the earth that can show the king's matter ... there is none other that can show it before the king, except the gods, whose dwelling is not with flesh" (Daniel 2.1-11).

"The gods" here symbolise *psychic consciousness*, containing the wisdom of the archtypes which Nebuchadnezzar at that time knew nothing of, being blinded by his own superego-consciousness, identified with his own temporal power as the head of a society that had so recently had such great cultural and military success that it had been able to destroy the temple at Jerusalem and take large numbers of the Jews captive.

The account goes on:—

"For this cause the king was angry and very furious, and commanded to destroy all the wise men of Babylon" (Daniel 2.12).

Among these wise men was Daniel, one of the four Hebrew youths previously selected by the master of Nebuchadnezzar's eunuchs for their integrity and "cunning in knowledge", the other three being the famous Shadrach, Meshach and Abed-nego, whom Nebuchadnezzar subsequently threw into the burning, fiery furnace but who were not burnt (Daniel 1.3–17 and 3). Daniel was thus externally the head of a quaternity of god-fearing young men who together constitute a Self in the psychological sense, and were in touch with "God", symbolising that fifth overall function which we call psychic consciousness.

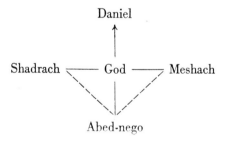

Figure 5

Shadrach, Meshach and Abed-nego are what are sometimes called "The Three Children", who were cast into the fiery furnace because they would not bow down to the image of gold which Nebuchadnezzar set up. But the fire did not consume them. A fourth man appeared with them whose form was "like the Son of God" (Daniel 3.25). Together with Daniel these made five, of which God was the quintessence. Later Daniel himself was cast into the den of lions, but he also survived unhurt (Daniel 6.22).

Daniel did not act alone in his hope to preserve his life, but consulted the three others, the four together enfolded in God symbolising the totality of human psychic consciousness. They all four prayed, and it was only in response to this that "Then was the secret revealed unto Daniel in a night vision" (Daniel 2.19), and he approached the king saying, "there is a God in heaven who revealeth secrets, and maketh known to the king Nebuchadnezzar what shall be in the latter days", humbly declaring "But as for me, this secret is not revealed to me for any wisdom that I have more than any living, but . . . that thou mightest know the thoughts of thine heart."

Then Daniel told the king what the king's own dream-vision had been, which he had forgotten, but which Daniel now also saw, and did not forget because he understood. "Thou, O king, sawest, and behold, a great image. . . . whose brightness was excellent . . . ; and the form thereof was terrible. This image's head was of fine gold, his breast and his arms of silver, his belly and his thighs of brass, his legs of iron, his feet part of iron and part of clay."

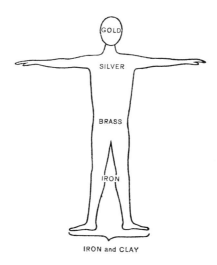

Figure 6

It will be noted that there are here five substances, four metals and one of clay, described as six (the iron being mentioned twice), all contained in the seventh, the image itself. But there was another seventh substance, which was opposed to the image. For Daniel then went on:—

"Thou sawest till that a stone was cut out without hands, which smote the image upon his feet that were of iron and of clay, and brake them to pieces."

"Then was the iron, the clay, the brass, the silver, and the gold, broken to pieces together, and became like the chaff of the summer threshing-floors; and the wind carried them away, that no place was found for them: and the stone that smote the image became a great mountain, and filled the whole earth" (Daniel 2.31–35).

Analytical Parallel
Daniel as Psychotherapist

Let us first ask ourselves what was meant by Nebuchadnezzar forgetting his own dream, but Daniel "seeing" the same vision and not forgetting it, and being able to interpret it.

Phenomena such as this are not confined to biblical times. It is a fact of personal experience, of a kind that may well open our eyes to what the Bible really is saying, that, even today, when, in psychological analysis, a patient has got stuck, and the analyst has got stuck too, this indicating that both their ego-consciousnesses have failed to follow the trail of the archetypal process incubating in the patient's psyche, something remarkable sometimes happens.

If both can be for a while silent in the attempt to cast off pre-conceived ideas, then, sooner or later, dream-visions may come, either to both of them, or to the analyst only as being more adept at getting into touch with psychic consciousness. Such visions may at first sight seem to be purely personal, as touching only on the individual problems of either patient or analyst. But when they are expressed in words a truly remarkable phenomenon reveals itself. Either each one has had what is essentially the same visionary experience, or else, when the analyst says what his vision has been, the patient may reply that just that thought or feeling symbolised by the vision had been in his or her mind too, but had appeared either irrelevant or not worth mentioning.

What has in fact happened is that the blockage that had occurred in both their ego-consciousnesses had been a common one, and that the solution has come through the operation of something that is at once personal and archetypal, a power acting *through* man, but not *of* man, delivering a common message to any two such persons through the medium of each one's personal associations and quite separate personality. In this way the personal channels differ, according to each one's personal experience and life history, but the message is the same because life's deepest problems are in the main the same for everyone.

Experiences of this kind are proof that there is such a thing as psychic consciousness, and that it can be relied on to suggest solutions to otherwise insoluble problems. Naturally, it is something that has to be worked for, which has its possibility of deception in inexperienced hands, and the encounter with which is at first disturbing. The analyst may well ask himself, "Is this *my* personal vision only, or what is it? If I use it, am I not running the risk of projecting my own psychology and problems on to the patient who has quite different ones? Is this not illegitimate, and, if so, highly harmful, causing the patient's problem to be contaminated by the analyst's, and so leading both analyst and patient astray?"

Such questions are essential, and the analyst to whom such experience is new must indeed be on his guard. It may take years to come to terms with it. But, with the proviso that one is ceaselessly self-critical, whatever personal affects intrude may with enough diffidence be sorted out, and the core of truth be seized that in fact archetypal messages of this kind do come through, which can on the whole be trusted, if they are taken with the saving and quite necessary grace of humour, based on the knowledge that such happenings are mysteries; mysteries, not in the false sense of being beyond comprehension, but in the true sense that they are revelations, which become less and less mysterious in the "spooky" sense the more familiar we come to be with them. If they are understood in this way, and always with a grain of salt, they become no more mysterious than how we digest our food or how we breathe. Such physical processes are mysteries indeed, but they are mysteries which we can use and trust, without quite knowing how they come about. The same applies to the visions produced by psychic consciousness, if once we grasp that they convey messages from a power wiser than ego-consciousness, and underlying all ego-consciousness.

"*Thou art this head of gold*"
The four "kingdoms"

Daniel proceeds to analyse the king's dream as any analyst might when seeking to impress a new patient relating a first dream with the reality of psychic consciousness which is expressed in it. He also uses the time-worn technique of first agreeing, and almost flattering, before venturing to criticise. He says: "Thou, O king, art a king of kings: for the God of heaven hath given thee a kingdom, power, and strength, and glory. And wheresoever the children of men dwell, the beasts of the field and the fowls of the heaven hath he given into thine hand, and hath made thee ruler over them all. *Thou art this head of gold**."

He thus refers to the king's so-called "superior" function, the super-ego which, it will be noted, is the superior function not only of kings but of all humanity.

This dream of Nebuchadnezzar's was thus not only his own. It was known to Daniel, for he saw it. And it is also ours. Its imagery is set in terms of Nebuchadnezzar's royal state, and of the god in whom he put his trust. But its content applies to all humanity, with the four main psychological functions which all of us have, which Daniel now proceeds to refer to as four "kingdoms". The head of gold symbolises the superior function or "kingdom". Daniel goes on: "And after thee shall rise another kingdom inferior to thee", referring to the silver one (the breast and arms), "and another third kingdom of brass, which shall bear rule over all the earth", referring in body-image symbolism to the belly and

---

* My italics.

the thighs, symbolising the so-called "lower" emotions. These do indeed rule over all the earth, replenishing it physically with the seed of man. But the mystery lies not in them.

The mystery lies in the fourth function, symbolised by the legs made of iron, and the feet, part of iron and part of clay, that part of the body-image on which we stand and move, which is dual and thus contains the possibility of transformation. In order to be transformed, things have to break. This is the motive of dismemberment and consequently of sacrifice. Thus Daniel reaches his climax:

"And the fourth kingdom shall be as strong as iron: forasmuch as iron breaketh in pieces and subdueth all things, shall it break in pieces and bruise."

"Bruising." The Iron and the Clay
The psychic "seed of man"

Bruising recalls Genesis, when God cursed the serpent and said of the woman and her seed (her progeny) that "it shall bruise thy head, and thou shalt bruise his heel" (Gen. 3.15). So, in Daniel's interpretation of Nebuchadnezzar's dream, the whole image is to be bruised, beginning with the feet of iron and of clay. For "Whereas thou sawest the feet and toes, part of potter's clay, and part of iron, the kingdom shall be divided: but there shall be in it of the strength of the iron, forasmuch as thou sawest the iron mixed with miry clay. And as the toes of the feet were part of iron, and part of clay, so the kingdom shall be partly strong, and partly broken."

We may well ask what this means. Biblical critics have advanced all sorts of historical and mystical theories. But if we read closely, and with our eyes on matter-of-fact everyday human relationships, we need not wonder overmuch. For he goes on now to explain in terms of everyday kinship: "And whereas thou sawest iron mixed with miry clay, they shall mingle themselves with the *seed of men* [my italics]: but they shall not cleave to one another, even as iron is not mixed with clay."

We shall see later (pp. 304, 317–24, 325, 334) what "iron" and "clay" mean in the male-female sense. What is to be transformed here is "the seed of men", which is the human *prima materia*, taken in the psychic sense in which the Bible always takes it. For the iron and clay associated with the seed of men together constitute the complex fourth function, of which Daniel now says: "And in the days of those kings shall the God of heaven set up a kingdom, which shall never be destroyed: and the kingdom shall not be left to other people, but it shall break in pieces and consume all these kingdoms, and it shall stand for ever."

What stands for ever is *prima materia* spiritualised, "the seed of men" transformed, matter or appearances which perish or fade away turned into spirit which perishes not and is the seed of immortality. I here suggest that "the kingdom shall not be left to other people" means that the psyche shall not be projected on to other people, or on to society, for it is now within. It is the kingdom of heaven *within*, which, as we are told in the New Testament, cannot perish. It is "the kingdom *without*" which perishes, or must be "broken" so that the *inward* kingdom may arise.

Daniel goes on to explain what brings such transformation about: "Forasmuch as thou sawest that the stone was cut out of the mountain without hands, and that it break in pieces the iron, the brass, the clay, the silver, and the gold; the great God hath made known to the king what shall come to pass hereafter: and the dream is certain, and the interpretation thereof sure" (Daniel 2.37–45).

"Judgment"

Here God is represented as a judge. But Justice has two sides. Justice is stern, but at the same time traditionally represented as blindfold, impartial some might say, but others might say merciful. It is well known that Mithra as a god looks the other way while slaying the bull of his own untransformed nature because it is too difficult to face directly, and that Perseus turned his head away from the gaze of Medusa while cutting off her head. Thus transformation has two sides, a male or stern one, an archetypal quality of certainty, the certainty of doom, the terrifying "last judgment" that saves, and another human quality of merciful acceptance, enabling the sufferer, through submitting to it, to come through his suffering to a realisation of truth that transcends it.

In the dialectic between the two biblical protagonists, Nebuchadnezzar and Daniel, we may perceive these two aspects of judgment. For the name Nebuchadnezzar means philologically "tears and groans of judgment", "trouble", or "sorrow of judgment" (see Cruden's Concordance). He is one who is made to suffer in ego-consciousness, and, as we shall see, becomes transformed through his suffering.

The name Daniel means "God is judge, judgment of God" or "God is my judge", and is thus based on the same concept of justice seen by him from the angle of psychic consciousness. For the suffix "-el" is the same as that found in the word *elohim,* the primitive plural signifying the duality of God, a word familiar to us also in the Muslim name *Allah.* The name Daniel may thus be compared with those of the archangels Michael and Gabriel, both of whom appear for the first, and almost only, time in the book of Daniel, and with both of whom he converses:— Michael, whose name means "Who is like God?", and is referred to as a "prince" or a "great prince" (Daniel 10.13, 21; 12.1), and Gabriel, whose name means "God is my strength", whom Daniel speaks of simply as a "man" (Daniel 8.16; 9.21). All these thus symbolise potential human qualities, derived from archetypal source. Daniel is one of them, and though a vehicle for "prophecy", which literally means "inspired word", is also represented biblically as a man, appearing only in the book of dream interpretation which is called after him.

It is thus relevant in this context to know what the concept "judgment", found in the names of both Daniel and Nebuchadnezzar, and which often sounds to us so frighteningly impersonal, actually means. The English word "judge" comes from the Latin stem *iū-dic,* signifying "one who points out the law" (Skeat). But law, like judgment, has two sides to it. There is man's law, and what is called God's law. Man's law may be equated with the rules and conventions of society, and in the individual with the superego. In the dialectic between Nebuchadnezzar and Daniel, this would be symbolised by the golden image which Nebuchadnezzar set up, and which he commanded to be worshipped as, we may say, an image of himself as the head of society. God's law is, on the contrary, to be equated with psychic consciousness, which is the hidden complementary opposite, expressed in the words uttered by Daniel.

The four-fold Tables of the Law (the "stone" uniting them), and the Four-section Kinship System

Though there were prophets in those days, and though the prophets may have denounced the kings, we must not take this too literally as an external confrontation only between two persons, but rather as an internal confrontation between two forces operating at once in society and also in each individual.

The biblical symbolism for this dichotomy is the "two tables of the law", also called the "two tables of testimony", written on the two "tables of stone" which God gave to Moses.

These tables constituted, however, not a simple duality, for "the tables were written on both their sides; on the one side and on the other side". And "the tables were the work of God, and the writing was the writing of God, graven upon the tables" (Exod. 32.15–16). The two tables were thus complementary opposites, and each table contained yet further its own internal opposite, thus making a quaternity, with God as the fifth or quintessence, originating and ruling them all.

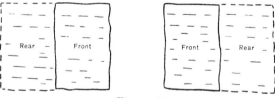

Figure 7

The two stone "tables of the law", or tables of "testimony" constituting a basic duality, which, since they were both written on both sides, turns out in fact to be a quaternity. The stone, engraved by God, may be equated with the philosopher's stone, and also with the stone "cut without hands" of Nebuchadnezzar's dream.

Both "stone" and God are the quintessential elements embracing the four messages, which were originated by God and contained in the stone.

It has been mentioned already how primitive society was also organised on a four-fold basis, formed by the interaction of the matrilineal and patrilineal moieties, producing two sets of conscious and unconscious motivations in each of the two sexes, and in society as a whole, in which marriages are regulated according to rules governing the relations between kinship sections, rather than by the choice of individuals.

Since each individual is a part of this four-fold society, each member of it also carries in himselfs or herself this same four-fold psychic imprint. We cannot therefore escape the conclusion that the tables of the law were on the same model as that of a marriage between the sister-exchanging couples in a primitive four-section kinship system, each of which two simultaneous marriages has its own conscious and contra-sexually unconscious aspect, corresponding respectively to ego-consciousness with its complementary opposite, psychic consciousness. The four are united in "God", represented externally by the basically four-fold society in which all are contained, and to maintain which all live their social lives.

The symbolism of the stone tables may be carried yet further if we consider that, God being "all" and therefore male and female, his female aspect may well be symbolised by the stone itself on which all four interlacing truths or "laws" or "testimonies" are written by him in his male aspect; the two together, like society, embracing all. The graven stone is thus also equatable with the philosopher's stone of alchemy, which is the quintessence of the four-fold division of the *prima materia* which constitutes the Self in its most primitive female-male aspect.

The Stone "cut out without hands"
The Iron and Clay "mingle" but do not "cleave"
Incest Taboo and Sacrifice

Being psychic and not material, the stone tables are equatable also with the "stone cut out without hands" of Nebuchadnezzar's and Daniel's common night-time vision, indicating spirit transcending the four separate functions with their possibilities of union-in-opposition, which the tables of the stone unite. In terms of different aspects of maleness, the graven stone may thus be thought of as symbolising at once the Father and the Son, the Father in that by graving and thus penetrating it and dividing it into four gives rise to consciousness, and the "child" or Son that has at last been born from it, and manifests this consciousness, these being in fact two aspects of one male influence in the way that Christ is said to have created Mary and thus fathered her in order to bear him as her son.

This symbolises the psychic "seed of men" which Daniel refers to as arising from the mingling of "iron and miry clay", the iron mined out of the earth being another symbol for the spirit extracted from the flesh symbolised by the miry clay, but in such a way that "they shall not cleave to one another, even as iron is not mixed with clay". For, as should be emphasised, in the symbolism of the Bible as a psychological document, "man" means not physical man but man's psyche; the whole biblical theme being that a man should cease to be "mere man" but, as stated as early as in the second chapter of Genesis (verse 7), should become "a living soul".

This involves sacrifice, a word now often so masochistically misunderstood that it has lost most of its meaning as a highly practical measure leading to greater happiness and the overcoming of hindrances that otherwise hamper us. Sacrifice does not mean the giving up or abandonment of good things that *still* are good. What it does mean is not being deluded by the belief that what was once good will always remain so. For life moves on. It means the letting go, for the sake of transforming it, of something that was indeed once of supreme value, like the mother-child relationship which is at first life-giving, a matter of life and death to the infant at its mother's breast. But if it continues too long it becomes a death-trap of self-destruction.

The "Mother" untransformed, that is uninfluenced by the father-principle, may be equated with "nature". The same applies, therefore, also to man's identification with his own nature, identified with his own inalienable rightness, which is essential for the infant to be allowed to have, but which later prevents growth in adulthood, and must be modified by other considerations if the psyche is to develop alongside nature as an *alter ego* or "second self". Thus *sacer,* from which we derive the word "sacrifice", means "set apart", as in the case of the iron and miry clay of Nebuchadnezzar's dream, which "mingle" but do not "cleave". For the one must be able to see the other one, as female and male, as ego-consciousness perceptive of psychic consciousness. While both exist in the same person, each must be able to recognise the other's independent co-existence, which cannot happen if they "cleave", which means to remain undifferentiated and thus mother- (nature-) bound and psychologically incestuous.

The "doubling" of Nebuchadnezzar and of Job through the addition of psychic consciousness based on the father-principle

Nebuchadnezzar was to have several shattering experiences, including yet another dream, before he ceased identifying himself with psychic consciousness mistakenly externalised as superego in the form of worldly supremacy, presumptuously acting as the personification of society, saying, "Is not this great Babylon, that I have built for the kingdom by the might of my power, and for the honour of my majesty?".

But he was to be transformed. For "while the word was in the king's mouth, there fell a voice from heaven, saying, O king Nebuchadnezzar, to thee it is spoken; the kingdom is departed from thee. And they shall drive thee from men, and thy dwelling shall be with the beasts of the field: they shall make thee to eat grass as oxen, and seven times shall pass over thee, until thou know that the most High ruleth in the kingdom of men, and giveth it to whomsoever he will." Note here the number seven, associated with Nebuchadnezzar's presumptuous self-identification with the deity (the seven-fold configuration in Figure 4).

But he was humbled, for "The same hour was the thing fulfilled upon Nebuchadnezzar: and he was driven from men, and did eat grass as oxen, and his body was wet with the dew of heaven, till his hairs were grown like eagles' feathers, and his nails like birds' claws."

"And at the end of the days I Nebuchadnezzar lifted up mine eyes unto heaven, and mine understanding returned unto me, and I blessed the most High, and I praised and honoured him that liveth for ever, whose dominion is an everlasting dominion." Then, and only then, "the glory of my kingdom, mine honour and brightness returned unto me; and my counsellors and my lords sought unto me; and I was established in my kingdom, and excellent majesty was added unto me".

"Now I Nebuchadnezzar praise and extol and honour the King of heaven, all whose works are truth, and his ways judgment" (Daniel 4.30–37).

The key words for our understanding here are "judgment", "everlasting dominion", "kingdom" and the small word "added". For of the two main psychological kingdoms, or spheres of operation, the external and the internal, the external has to be built first, as a containing mother, in order to incubate the inner one. But the external mother-kingdom then has to go, so that the inner kingdom may flourish and free itself. Then the external kingdom may return, not as the dominating mother, but as the serving one, the servant and not the mistress of the new-born spirit of the individual, that ultimate aim which some call "God", others *mana,* which we here think of as psychic consciousness. It is the complement to ego-consciousness, which only flourishes creatively if it enters into partnership with psychic consciousness by serving it, and acts as its executive instead of trying to dominate, enslave or suppress it. Psychic consciousness then becomes as it were the well from which ego-consciousness may drink, and which supplies it with wisdom.

Thus Nebuchadnezzar's sacrifice, involuntary though it was, once he had accepted this blessing in disguise of thoroughly experiencing the bestial nature of inflation through self-identification with society as a kind of deity, was the means of his being re-admitted into life, not deprived but *doubled,* with psychic consciousness added, as Job was "doubled" after his trials, as a result of which "the Lord gave Job twice as much as he had before" (Job 42.10).

The necessary destruction

Before this happened, however, the iron, the clay, the brass, the silver, and the gold of Nebuchadnezzar's image of himself as the mighty one, had to be broken, and "the wind carried them away, that no place was found for them". So also the tree of Nebuchadnezzar's second dream which "reached unto heaven" had to be cut down (Daniel 4.10 ff.). Even the tables of the law, which God had given to Moses, had to be broken as Moses "brake them beneath the mount" (Exod. 32.19), the golden calf had to be burnt, and the Children of Israel stripped until they were naked (Exod. 32.25), and every Levite had to slay "his brother, and every man his companion, and every man his neighbour", until it came to be known, as Moses said "Who is on the Lord's side?". They even had to slay their sons: "And there fell of the people that day about three thousand men. For Moses had said, "Consecrate yourselves to day to the Lord, even every man upon his son, and upon his brother; that he may bestow upon you a blessing this day" (Exod. 32.26–29).

We may think of this as of that form of willing human sacrifice that Abraham was prepared to make of his love for his son Isaac, the sacrifice of the most beloved, comparable to primitive sacrifice of the consecrated animal symbolising self-regard, through sacrifice of which the consecration devolves on the sacrificer (see Layard, 1955, p. 18; 1956, p. 383).

Not till these things were done in the desert, did God show Moses his "back parts" and tell him then to "hew ... two tables of stone like unto the first: and I will write upon those tables the words that were in the first tables, which thou brakest" (Exod. 33.23; 34.1), saying "Behold, I make a covenant: before all thy people I will do marvels, such as have not been done in all the earth, ... for it is a terrible thing that I will do with thee". And "thou shalt worship no other god: for the Lord, whose name is Jealous, is a jealous God", for which, in the English language, the doublet, spelt with a "z", is "zealous", from the Greek ζῆλος meaning "zeal" or "ardour", yielding the two opposites of the Spanish *celoso*, "jealous", and the Late Latin *zēlōsus*, "full of zeal".

Both words well describe the operation of psychic consciousness, which, if a man heed it, gives him dynamic force and real personality, but if not heeded by ego-consciousness will render him as stupid as an ox, and hiddenly dangerous as a bird of prey with claws, whereby he loses personality and becomes a tool of the most retrograde forces, however brilliant he may be or apparently god-fearing.

III.

MALEKULAN

Transition
The primitive meaning of "stone"
Earth symbolising the Soul

Let us now take an example from Malekula to show how this dream of Nebuchadnezzar's is a very condensed illustration of the conflict between ego-consciousness and psychic consciousness, which all primitive peoples as well as ourselves are engaged in, whether we will or no.

Nebuchadnezzar's image of himself symbolises a concept of society which, though basically necessary for human development, has nevertheless overreached itself. Society functions as an "externalised psyche" (see page 12 and general theme of Layard, 1945, and Jung's *Psychology of the Transference*, Collected Works, vol. 16) which may be satisfactory enough as a collective framework, so long as it is not allowed to become a tyrant sapping the individual of his individuality, thus stultifying the spirit which in the first place gives rise to it, and which should properly arise from it anew in each member of it that is born. Human nature is, however, so conservative that this often does not happen and individuality thus gets repressed.

This being so, successive re-formations have to take place, the impetus for which arises, not in those who have been able to "fit in" most easily with society with the misleadingly false sense of psychic security which it is apt sometimes to give, but in those whom it irks and have the good fortune to collapse as Nebuchadnezzar did, or otherwise find their way to psychic consciousness through suffering understood, with or without external help.

The saving action always begins with destruction, the destruction of ideals that are untenable or too restricted. It may appear at first to the individual victim of this destruction that it is senseless, and, if he resent too much, he will be destroyed. But the agent of destruction is not an enemy. It is a friend. In the case of a quaternity it is the third, fifth or seventh function (all odd numbers) that centralises the other two, four, or six, as the case may be, and has the power over them to destroy in order to build them up again in a new pattern. The destruction is only an apparent one, designed to internalise what had formerly been externalised, in other words to "buy back" the soul which had depended on outside things and people, so as to integrate it internally, where alone it can become pregnant for the individual and give birth to spirit, and at the same time immortality.

The active "fifth thing" was, in Nebuchadnezzar's dream, the "stone" not made with hands, that "smote the image" and "became a great mountain, and filled the whole earth". The "whole earth" here means the "whole personality", which thus becomes progressively more filled with spirit, which we have equated with the philosopher's stone and with *mana*, such as is thought in the megalithic culture of Malekula to have its first dwelling in stone, stone being the only—or almost only—incorruptible form of matter in the hot, steamy Malekulan tropics, where metal is unknown and all human artifacts, including houses or even statues made of wood, so quickly decay. It is for this reason that the stone monuments are erected in honour of the ancestors, in which their spirits dwell, so as to give them an imperishable house, so that man's spirit may not perish as the stone does not perish. For the spirits of the ancestors symbolise collectively the spirit of the tribe, they being the upholders of its moral code, visiting offenders with death and other penalties.

There is a dual meaning in all this, for the stones thus erected are thought to be "persons" in the sense that the stones themselves are supposed, in their own natures, always to have had individuality, and even names, even while they were as yet lying unrecognised beneath the ground or on the coral reefs surrounding the islands. In this way they resemble the precious metals or stones of alchemy, which corresponded with the ruling planets and were their incarnation not *on* but *in* the earth. The Malekulans with their primitive megalithic culture have no planetary cosmology, but they have this concept of stones living in the earth, waiting to be "born" from it as from a womb when the time is ripe. Earth symbolises in this imagery the pregnant female soul of man, from which the male spirit symbolised by these stones is born.

The planets appeared to the alchemists to have individuality because, unlike the fixed stars, they move. But the stones which the Malekulans revere do not move themselves. They must be moved by man. The earth will not yield up her treasure nor "let her children go" until man labours to free the treasure from her maternal unconsciously withholding grasp. So it is man himself that in the end releases his own spirit symbolised by stone taken from the female earth symbolising his soul, which must be worked at so as to separate the spirit from the soul which otherwise will not yield it up.

Stones used as tombstones to mark men's graves also cover or contain the dead, so that the concepts of the spirits of the ancestors and stone are inextricably interwoven.

Another meaning for "stone" in this Malekulan context is that, being hard and unyielding, it is a symbol for the incest taboo, which is the basis of human society recognised as such so much more consciously by the primitives than it is by us because the urge to commit incest is still strong with them, and is the subject of much talk and thought, and is sometimes yielded to though much condemned. It is the worst possible offence from the ancestral spirits' point of view, and the symbol of incest infuses their whole mythology.

The psychological equivalent to incest on the level of ego-consciousness is self-regard, the sin which Nebuchadnezzar and Job were most guilty of in the form of identification with a rigidly righteous social law.

It is this identification with the social system as a containing "male mother" that has to be destroyed, or at least modified, if the individual, and indeed society itself, is to be saved from such self-righteousness. This is what basically has both to be built up and sacrificed, in Malekula as in the Bible and elsewhere.

Stone and Tusked Boar
The Sister-Anima

The transformation process is most notable in Malekula where the sacrificial tusked boars symbolising incest, which may be social in the form of self-righteousness as well as corporal, are tied to the stone monuments in which the spirits of the ancestors dwell, so that the ancestors in the form of stone may witness the sacrifice. The culminating moment arrives when, as has been described elsewhere (*Identification with the Sacrificial Animal,* "Eranos-Jahrbuch" 1956, pp. 382ff.), at the moment of sacrifice the "spirit of the boar", which is the spirit of incest transformed into *mana,* "leaps out" and penetrates the sacrificer, as the boar's skull is cracked open to release it with a special wooden hammer which the sacrificer uses for the purpose. This hammer is itself carved to symbolise the power of transformed incest by being adorned with male and female images in divine embrace, indicating the *hieros gamos* resulting from the sacrifice.

When the boar is dead its flesh is eaten, not by the sacrificer, but by his male maternal relatives, to whom he owes this duty of rendering back to them what was theirs, namely the symbol of his own incest desire. But, when they have eaten it, they then return to him the lower jaw, which has in it the famous tusks which have been artificially elongated during the boar's life as part of the boar's consecration as a sacrificial divinity. For these are the boar's imperishable part, symbolising the spirit which grows out of the boar's body as the male child grows out of the mother and finally separates itself from her.

The symbolism is the same as that of the stone extracted from the earth. The tusk symbolises the spiritual essence of the boar, that part of the boar which does not decay, and is the nearest thing to what we call a "jewel" that the Malekulan can possess.

Thus also the man, in renouncing incest, acquires, instead of a sister-wife, an anima. As the external marriage between male and female gives rise to the child, so inwardly, as a result of this change, the "child" or progeny of the resulting *hieros gamos* is the *mana* which the Malekulan thus acquires, which gives him his "doubled life", the life of ego-consciousness joined to psychic consciousness, or maleness joined to femaleness, to which he thus attains.

The Spirit and the Withholding Soul
Psychic life here and now

The answer to the question *si jeunesse savait, si vieillesse pouvait* is thus not so obscure to the Malekulan as it is for some of us, since, like the Hebrew and the Babylonian, he has no doubt about the afterlife, which is not what we think of as something only "afterwards in time" but with the concept "after" used in the same sense in which we use it in the nautical expression "fore and aft", aft meaning the stern or rear end of a ship which guides it though the bow seems to lead. What is called "afterlife" is thus a symbol not only for the future but, much more basically, for the function of *mana* here and now, which means for psychic consciousness as opposed to ego-consciousness which only acts as its executive. For "after" means "behind". A ship is steered from behind, as unseen psychic consciousness steers ego-consciousness in the right direction to the extent that it is effectively in touch with it. If the individual does not make or loses contact with it, he psychically dies. This is expressed in Malekula by the mythological belief that his spirit after death will be devoured by the Great Mother in her negative aspect as the well-known Female Devouring Ghost. It will thus be annihilated, so that it no longer lives. As we might put it, this mythological figure in her negative aspect symbolises the withholding soul, the opposite of the receptive soul, jealously preventing psychic development.

Since it is the spirit only which survives after death, it is thus spoken of often in terms of future life. But every Malekulan knows that it is something that grows during *this* life out of the sacrificial process, which is the equivalent to the destruction of mother-son identity and to its replacement by reaching out towards the father-world, symbolised in Malekula as the spirit of male ancestors which constitute collectively what we would call the psychic consciousness of the tribe, on whose good will each living member of the tribe depends. These are those ancestors who have in their past lives overcome the Great Mother in her negative aspect, whereon she turns to them her positive aspect, and receives them back into her most creative womb, symbolised by the fire on the volcano where they live in everlasting union as her son-lovers and fathers.

We cannot get away, in speaking of psychic things, from sexual analogy, which is at the same time social analogy. For incest and the incest taboo on which society is founded are complementary opposites, which the Malekulan is much more conscious of than we are, since he is closer to nature, and incest is natural.

An ego knowing this is founded in reality, a word which in our own language comes from the late Latin *reālis* meaning "belonging to the thing itself" (Skeat), from Latin *res*, "a thing", which is significantly feminine. Matter, related to *mater* meaning "mother", is symbolically feminine, as is all *prima materia*. The Greek word ψυχή, indicating psychic substance or soul-stuff, is also feminine, corresponding to the Latin *anima*.

This brings us to the "two laws" again, both "mother" laws, those of material nature and of psychic substance or soul-stuff, which is also feminine. The function of psychological masculinity, that is to say psychic consciousness, is to pierce in between these two aspects of femininity, so as to know them both and thus not to be bound by both, but, as a centralising *third* thing, to move freely between them.

Sister-exchange and the four-section kinship system
The All-Father and the lack of recognised ancestors

Psychic consciousness is based on sex consciousness. It is internally hermaphrodite, modelled on that inner phallic urge towards femininity which sex is founded on, diverted by the incest taboo to seek ever wider fields of exploration to compensate for plain incest, which means non-differentiation in the choice of a mate and in sex fantasy.

Those who have followed earlier communications on primitive four-section kinship organisation will remember how this is based on the two exogamous matrilineal moieties containing two opposite kinds of women, those whom a man may marry, and those whom he may not. These symbolise basically the "two laws".

The women of one moiety are those who, in a purely matrilineal system, he may marry, and thus carry no incest taboo. The women of the other moiety, which is his own including his mother and sister, are the objects of the incest taboo creating the frustration which diverts incest desire into those psychic channels of internal fantasy that, if accepted positively as a blessing in disguise and thus not rejected, form the basis of psychic consciousness.

The collective manifestation of this is tribal mythology, which owes its existence to the incest taboo as the dynamic third factor in this sociological triad. There forms itself at the same time a personal psychological triad in each individual, with basic sexuality as its moving force and incest frustration as its transforming one.

The frustration has its sociological compensation and ultimate purpose in the formation of society, ruled by the father-principle which instituted the taboo, as opposed to the mother-principle, the "natural" one which it is the work of the father-principle to transform and as a social factor to regulate. Its psychological compensation is the development of psychic consciousness, due to the transformation of nature internally, leading in Malekulan belief to immortality when the shell of the body, having achieved its purpose, decays while psychic consciousness lives on. Psychic consciousness, thus basically "male", is what survives, in unity with transformed femininity, as the spirits of the ancestors, whose home is in the fiery volcano which is the Fire of the Great Devouring Mother who is now subdued and in the service of man rather than against him, at the same time live on in the hearts of men to strengthen them and ultimately to become one with them.

But the existence of these ancestors as historical figures, the memory of whose lives and exploits persists in native tradition alongside their archetypal significance as builders-up of the collective tribal psychic consciousness, is due to yet another social upheaval.

The old four-section kinship system depending on sister-exchange marriage had to be disrupted for sexual libido to be freed enough from the control of children by parents for psychic consciousness to develop as its internal parallel. For in that system, as explained elsewhere, two parent couples, of which the husbands had themselves, through the socially approved action of their own parents, been forced to exchange their sisters for their wives, in turn constrained their children to do the same by arranging that each man's son should marry the other one's daughter, giving that son's sister in exchange to be married to the other one's son.

This system of sister-exchange marriage repeated generation after generation had the automatically mathematical result of producing two exogamous patrilineal moieties as well as matrilineal moieties, the crossing of which gave rise to the four exogamous kinship sections, in which a man could marry a woman belonging to one section only out of the four, even when he grew up and was in a position to choose a second or third wife for himself.

This had the effect of producing a number of very small closed "circular" or mandala-like kinship systems each repeating themselves every second generation, which were so near-incestuous that there was no room for "ancestry" beyond the second generation and there were thus no recognised ancestors. Their place was taken in Australia by a mythological All-Father, who, as the spirits of all ancestors rolled into one, symbolised the moral law and was the basic supporter of the incest taboo, which, in a four-section system, was thus, with the All-Father supporting it, the hidden fifth function.

What is hidden in overt life turns into the strength of the inner life. It is equivalent to what we call "conscience" which, rightly conceived, is not a hindrance but a door-opener to that inner world, enriched by fantasy and expressing itself in individual as well as tribal mythology which is the imagery with which psychic consciousness expresses itself.

Mythological
(collective tribal)
Fantasy

The All-Father in Australia. In Atchin the God of Light marries his only wife, Sister of the ten Stone Brothers symbolising the ten divisions of the tribe who are all one in Him (pp. 336 ff.).

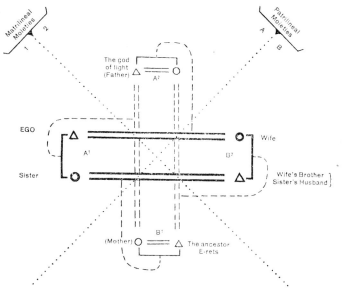

Personal Fantasy

E-rets marries Le-rets, his sister-anima (anima of the tribe).

Figure 8

Brackets indicate brother-sister pairs. Double lines indicate sister-exchange marriage in ego's own generation. Broken double lines indicate marriage between the other brother-sister pairs in the opposite alternating generations, whom ego may not marry. Broken single lines indicate descent (both ways) linking the four sections in the kinship system. Dotted lines show the division into matrilineal and patrilineal moieties giving rise to the four kinship sections A^1, A^2; B^1, B^2.

The diagram illustrates the mythological (tribal) and personal fantasies connected with the incest taboo which transform incest desire into *mana* or psychic consciousness.

Figure 8 is an attempt to link up kinship with psychic consciousness and with the imagery in which it is expressed, by showing how forbidden marriages develop their counterpart in those internal fantasies, tribal and individual, which have as their object the compensation of frustration by the growth of *mana* which is the ultimate object or final cause of the incest taboo. For the sake of economy in printing and in space, reference is made in it not only to the All-Father of Australian mythology, but also to myths connected with the various phases of *hieros gamos* in Atchin mythology which will be referred to later on pages 328ff. and 336ff. resulting from the break-up of the sister-exchanging system so as to produce an "open" system with greater scope for individuality than is possible in a closed one.

For psychic consciousness is so closely bound up in primitive existence with both sex and society, which are its twin external expressions, that, to expand, restrictions imposed on marriage must somehow be overcome and necessary adjustments made in order to encourage the concretization of sex fantasy and thereby enlarge society.

Disruption of the sister-exchanging system in favour of an open one giving more scope to individuality

I have described elsewhere[5] how the first movement towards such expansion in that part of Melanesia with which I am familiar was the evolution from four kinship sections into six, producing a six-section system, which still, however, was based on sister-exchange.

The next movement that we know of was the more recent one referred to in an article (1958) published in the volume called *Geist und Werk*[6] presented to Dr. Brody in his honour, and in gratitude for all the work which he has done, particularly for Eranos. This dealt with a period in Atchin history when the kinship system based on six sister-exchanging sections was being disrupted, as Nebuchadnezzar's six-fold image of

---
[5] 1945, pp. 277ff.
[6] *Geist und Werk*. Aus der Werkstatt unserer Autoren, zum 75. Geburtstag von Dr. Daniel Brody, Rhein-Verlag, Zurich 1958.

society and of his own psyche identified with it had to be broken up, and as the original four-fold tables of stone that Moses had received from God had to be broken up, so that they could be replaced by new ones.

The meaning of the social disruption as it occurred in the Small Islands of Malekula was that the sister-exchanging system, so necessary at first for social solidarity in very small communities struggling for their existence, was now proving too restrictive.

It was a system in which society was still far more important than the individual, and could in this way be likened to a "Mother" still possessing her "sons". The "sons" were all the men, who had to do what "Mother", in the form of society, told them to do in marrying a wife.

Such systems are indeed so closed that those within them are apt to equate the word "man" or "human being" with themselves, in such a way that those of other tribes with similar systems, with whom they come into occasional contact, are not thought of as "men", but as being outside the concept of "society" which applies only to themselves. Thus the word used for "man" means "man like me", belonging to my social circle and to no other. Viewed psychologically, this is "psychic incest", a kind of "primary narcissism" sociologically expressed. It signifies "man bound" within a social womb which is as essential to his welfare in this early cultural stage as are a mother's breasts to her child lest it die.

Homo-erotic consequence
Relationship with the bride's brother the basis of initiation and impregnation by the spirits of the ancestors

Such a restricted system has another consequence, as unintended by what we might think of as ego-consciousness in the form of society (though in fact caused by it) as a possessive mother's effect on her son's individual development. This is that, owing to the restricted choice of women for mating with, a youth may find himself betrothed to a girl still not nubile, or even as yet unborn, his father having contracted a marriage for him through agreement with his own bilateral first cousin, who promises to betroth the next daughter born to him to the first man's son. While the son is waiting for this girl to be born, or at least grow up so that she can be married to him, her parents will send her brother to be "married" to him in her stead. This brother serves as a stop-gap "wife" until his sister is nubile.

This is a custom recognised throughout Australia, in many parts of New Guinea and Melanesia, and elsewhere. Since bride and bride's brother both belong to the most opposite possible kinship section to ego, ego's relationship to them may be thought of as being on the same model as that of the relationship between ego-consciousness and psychic consciousness. Psychic consciousness being dual, it corresponds also to the "feet" made of iron and of clay in Nebuchadnezzar's dream-image of society mirrored in his own psyche, two substances which were contrasting hard and soft elements subject to change connected with the "seed of men".

The consequences of this bisexuality have been described in some detail in an article on *Homo-eroticism in Primitive Society as a Function of the Self* in the current issue of the "Journal of Analytical Psychology" (1959). The relevant fact here is that this primitive bisexuality ultimately resolves itself in initiation rites into a relationship between the tutor and his male novice calling one another respectively "husband" and "wife". Later still, the physical homosexual relationship between them disappears and is transmuted into a symbolic one in which it is no longer the tutor, but the spirits of the ancestors who are said symbolically to impregnate each novice in his feminine aspect with all the psychic knowledge of the tribe.

I will not here expand on this, as it can be read in that article. But it will be seen how, from a purely sexual beginning, arising out of sex frustration, a love relationship arises not only between men but at the same time between man and the spirits of the ancestors, who symbolise spirit in general and therefore psychic consciousness. It is a relationship which ego-consciousness is always apt to think of as suspect or somehow illegitimate, but which, if allowed to develop properly and not inhibited by false shame or its contrary, a secret conceit, in fact supports the highest interests both of the individual and society.

*Society as the "possessive mother" or externalised "withholding soul"
relaxes her grip
Newcomers challenge mothers' brothers and found patrilineages*

The homosexual relationship, having performed its function of giving rise to a psychic one, now recedes into the background, but not until something else has occurred to remove the cause of it, namely the abolition of sister-exchange marriages which in the first place gave rise to it.

As the grip of the "possessive mother" in this form relaxes, men now become more free to look around for other wives more suitable for their individual development. Society of course does not relax willingly, for this means challenge to parental restriction of the urge to mate, and to the whole social system that has produced this paradox.

It therefore leads to disruption from the point of view of the old form of society, before a new and wider social pattern is established to supersede the old. The old society naturally resists, and there is conflict.

In the social history of the small Malekulan island of Atchin, the young men now began to assert their right to have at least some say in the choice of a wife, and not to be bound either to marry their sister's husband's daughter, or necessarily give their sisters to be married to their wives' brothers. This social revolution coincided with the influx of new blood in the form of encroachment from outside by bands of men from a related but freer culture, making their way up the Malekulan coast towards the Small Islands, which, owing to their size, could conveniently contain just enough people—about 400—to maintain a closed sister-exchanging system in each of them, each such minute closed community having its own separate language.

The conflict took the form of combined envy of the newcomers' superior culture and wish to benefit by it, coupled with resistance to change. If, as I have elsewhere suggested, society may be regarded as a kind of "externalised soul", this is a picture of disturbance in the "withholding soul", externalised in the form of a rigid social order which was too near-incestuous, and therefore hampering to the individual. That this externalised soul was "female" there is no doubt, since its main defenders were the mothers' brothers (male representatives of the female line), who did not wish to see their daughters married to men over whom they had no control.

As opposed to this withholding soul in the form of a society resisting change, the threatening, and ultimately more powerful "spirit", was personified in the persons of the newcomers whose men-folk refused to be bound, but insisted on exercising freedom of choice in the selection of their brides.

The conflict with the mothers' brothers, whose daughters the newcomers married, brings out sharply the nature of the change that was taking place. This is well illustrated by the story told in *Geist und Werk* of the newcomer from the Malekulan mainland whose father had already married an Atchin woman but had not yet asserted his individuality sufficiently to change the Atchin social system, which in this instance took three generations to accomplish owing to the peculiar structure of it which will be described elsewhere in a larger book.

The hero of this story quarrelled with his elder brother on the Malekulan mainland, and took refuge from his brother's wrath by fleeing to his mother's brother's compound on Atchin, where he fell in love with a woman from another Atchin village whom her father had already betrothed, according to the old system, to another man. The newcomer contrived, however, to seduce her and finally to marry her.

This was against all precedent. Not only was it a marriage of comparatively free choice, but the old social system was challenged also in that, instead of taking his bride to live with him on Malekula, he went to live with her on Atchin in her own father's village, where he usurped her father's authority by founding a patrilineal lineage. This was a further innovation not possible under a system of sister-exchange marriage, which, with its equal weight given to both lines of descent in a closed "circular" kinship system, precludes the formation of lineages of any kind, whether patrilineal or matrilineal. Such systematised lack of differentiation was now disrupted by his action in usurping his wife's father's position of authority and founding patrilineal descent with himself at its head in his wife's father's village.

This, and similar marriages that were then taking place, gave the death-blow to the closed system of sister-exchange marriage.

The female "flesh and blood" and the male "bone"

To understand fully what had happened, and the connection with "the iron and the clay" (hard and soft substances) of Nebuchadnezzar's image, it may help us to recall the widespread primitive belief that, in the composition of the body, the flesh and the blood, which are the soft elements, are derived from the mother, while the bones, which are the "hard" elements, are thought of as a kind of congealed seminal substance connected with the marrow and the spinal cord derived from the father. The soft maternal elements, the flesh and the blood thus thought of as female and as the vehicle for the emotions, are subject to decay, while the hard elements, the bones connected with paternal begetting and mostly phallic in shape, are those parts of the body which survive for a considerable time after death, and are thus connected with immortality. In body-image symbolism, therefore, in which the body symbolises the whole psyche, the matrilineal line of flesh and blood symbolises, or is the carrier of, the soul which is female. The bones and patrilineal line of descent symbolise the spirit which is not only incubated in the soul but, like a skeleton, upholds it and gives it form, and subsequently outlives the soul, which, having performed its incubating function, dies, giving way to the male spirit which is at once its father and its child.

A third element intrudes
Bride-price in tusked boars replaces the sister given in exchange
The boar a symbol for incest
Three brothers-in-law replace two, leading to the foundation
of three patrilineages

It was the matrilineal element, split into matrilineal moieties, transmitted by the blood visible at childbirth, which fundamentally held the mandala-like sister-exchanging system together. The death of this system introduced the element of bride-price in the form of tusked boars paid by the man's family to the woman's family to replace the sister no longer given in exchange. Since this consists of wealth accumulated by the man's family by their work and inventiveness, it may well be thought of as symbolically a psychic substitute. Wealth that had been won from the earth in ever more and more complex ways as a result of man's psychic development, was paid back to the "earth", symbolised by the bride's family, for the acquisition of a wife.

In this new situation the third factor is the bride-price in the form of boars which was inserted, so to speak, as a wedge between the former sister-exchanging couples, dividing them in such a way as to destroy the near-incest of their previous relationship. The real intruder is the man, but the symbolic intruder is the sacrificial boar with its tusks symbolising sacrifice primarily of incest desire and in this case of near-incest, the boar being in place of the sisters who would formerly have been exchanged.

A further sacrifice of incest-boundness is the fact of free choice, in place of the parents' regulation of their sons' and daughters' marriages with the compulsory sister-exchange marriages previously arranged for them.

The sacrifice of the boar as symbol thus signifies a further extension of the incest taboo, and, with its tusk, corresponds to the stone which in Nebuchadnezzar's dream "smote the image", symbolising society, "upon his feet that were of iron and of clay, and brake them to pieces" so that the "iron and clay" connected with the "seed of man" "shall not cleave to one another, even as iron is not mixed with clay", and men no longer cleave to near-incest. The boar itself is sacrificed by being struck on the head, but, with its sacrifice, incest is also sacrificed through the separation of the former near-incest partners.

In this way the former social system founded on two matrilineal moieties and four kinship sections or multiples of two is shattered, and a basically three-fold system takes its place. For there are now not only two families involved who exchange sisters, but three who no longer

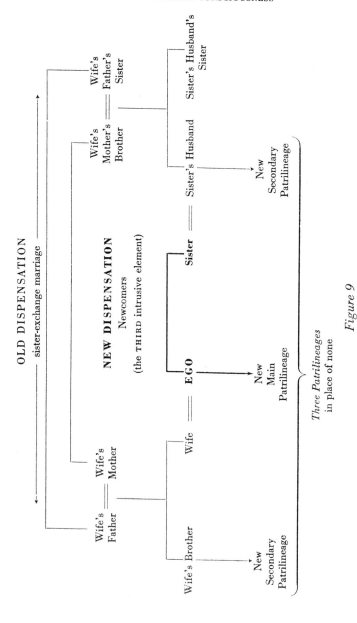

Figure 9

illustrating the break-up of sister-exchange marriage through the intrusion of a third element, giving rise to three patrilineages.

practise sister-exchange marriage. Each man, instead of having only one brother-in-law, who is at the same time his wife's brother and his sister's husband, has two brothers-in-law, one of whom marries his sister, and the other, his wife's brother, who marries someone else.

So there are now three brothers-in-law involved where formerly there were but two, each of the three now having his own patrilineage.

Comparative free choice. Detachment, "not cleaving"
Closed kinship system becomes an "open" one
Five patrilineages and the Pentacle
Five patri-villages. Odd and even numbers

Thus, out of the matrix or social womb of the former sister-exchanging system is born a "new thing", or shall we say a new thing arises, the spirit of man with an ego freed from the "cleaving together" of the "iron and clay" corresponding to the "bone and flesh" of near-incest marriages. The third thing thus beginning to make itself felt is the new element of free choice, the psychic element now released to some extent from the tyranny of possessive opposites, able to live its own life more independently.

This fosters a movement towards a feeling of "detachment" which the spirit needs to follow its own psychic laws, less dominated by social convention. On the analogy of the social system being an externalisation of the human psyche, it is a movement in the direction of freeing the spirit from the withholding soul.

Like all dynamic movements of the spirit, this new development had many results, both social and psychological.

Socially, it altered the whole pattern of society, not only making it three-fold but, owing to other factors mentioned in *Geist und Werk,* expanding it to be a five-fold one. For it will be noted that in Figure 9 the wife's brother and sister's husband's sister on either side of ego have no spouses allotted to them, each marrying some other relative who also has a brother or a sister married elsewhere, in such a way that in this new phase of kinship development there arise five patrilineages.

ON PSYCHIC CONSCIOUSNESS

These five then intermarry in the following way, causing a new and enlarged kinship connubium to arise on the following pattern which may be better seen in the diagram (Fig. 10) than if described in words.

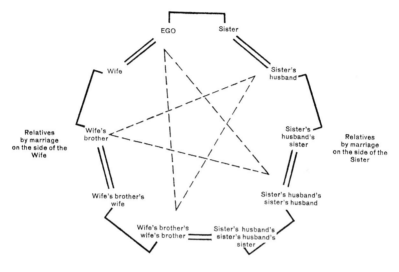

Figure 10

Simplified diagram of *five intermarrying patrilineages* organised into five patri-villages. Each brother-sister pair is bracketed. Double lines indicate marriage. Broken lines indicate the formation of the kinship pentacle.

Relatives by marriage on the sides of the wife and the sister respectively unite at the bottom of the diagram.

All those shown in the diagram are related in many other ways besides those of direct marriage. The relevant fact, however, is that each of the five men here indicated now has his own patrilineage, each patrilineage being at the same time patrilocal, that is to say each domiciled in its own separate village, called a patri-village because organised on a basis of patrilineal descent, making five patri-villages in all which together comprise the total population of Atchin.

This division into five villages or five patri-lineages, or patri-clans as they may be called if they are enlarged, is not confined to Atchin, but is basic over a large area at this stage of social development, when "closed" kinship systems based on sister-exchange marriage have begun to open their ranks and to become "open" ones not based on it.

It is a matter of pride for the Atchinese to vaunt that they are now a "five-fold" people, for which they use the mystic symbol of the pentacle, or five-pointed star drawn in a continuous line showing how the five patrilineages are all connected in a single kinship system on account of hidden alliances traced through the female line, which still binds them partially together, though it no longer rules.

Figure 11

The symbol of the Pentacle, as painted on the mask-banner of the Initiating Great Mother, indicating how the five patrilineages are all interrelated through the female line of descent.
It is thought of as a homunculus, with head, arms and legs.

As initiating symbol, the pentacle is one of the designs painted on the tall mask-banner representing the face and sharp-pointed "hat" of the Female Devouring Ghost or Initiating Great Mother, which is displayed to the novices on the completion of their initiation rites, when they are eventually released from their thirty-days' confinement in the initiation lodge, said to symbolise her "body" from which they now issue reborn.

Drawings of two such masks with the designs on them are to be seen in a former article on *The Making of Man in Malekula,* "Eranos-Jahrbuch" 1949, Figures 5a, 5b. Her purely female symbols are the moon, painted as a spiral in its three aspects as full moon, and waxing and waning (growing and dying), with a dark space on the mask symbolising her "death", equivalent to the novices' own "death" to the mother-world leading to their rebirth into the world of men and at the same time of incipient psychic consciousness.

As great Initiatrix, she is a Female Father figure who as serving the father-principle is revered, but as symbolising the devouring mother is feared till she is overcome, and is in this aspect symbolised as a shark said to attack the novices by trying to bite off their genitals, and as the night-hawk which swoops down at night to seize small unsuspecting animals. The mask symbolising her as such is formally shot at by the novices as their first act as young initiates, and thus destroyed, so as to show their conquest over her.

The pentacle, which is her "child", is also thought of as a homunculus with head, arms and legs, a little flying "man" who may be encountered anywhere, that is to say a psychic function, a notion not too far removed from the Greek concept of "psyche" as a butterfly with head, forewings and underwings, symbolising also a four-fold structure with the head as the quintessential function on which the other four depend, and at the same time leads. If we compare Figures 10 and 11, it will be noted that the significance of the "feet" of the homunculus symbolised by the pentacle is that, in the kinship system, this is the point at which ego's relatives by marriage on the side of the wife unite in marriage with those on the sister's side, thus creating a union of opposites similar to that of the "feet ... part of iron and part of clay" which do "not cleave to one another, even as iron is not mixed with clay" of Nebuchadnezzar's vision. What may not mix in the sphere of ego-consciousness is thus seen to unite in the opposing sphere of psychic consciousness, that is to say at the opposite end of the kinship connubium.

It is important therefore to remember that five, like three, is an odd number. Odd numbers are traditionally said to be symbolically "masculine", as opposed to even numbers which are symbolically "feminine". This is supported by the Malekulan evidence, which associates "five" with patrilineal descent. It is, moreover, "masculine" in another sense which is a psychic one, since odd numbers have a centre or "leader", which even numbers do not have. Thus two has no centre, and can be thought of only as symbolising the unresolved opposites. The same applies to four, which doubles two and has the opposites in two directions, but still has no centre.

On the other hand, the number three, considered structurally, consists of two opposites joined by a central third which unites them and leads. So also the fifth factor centrally unites and leads the two dichotomies of four. Psychologically, anything central implies individuality in the form of some kind of consciousness.

E-rets and Le-rets
The Culture-hero with his sister-wife
The Logos called "The Word"

It is thus not without interest that the chief Atchin culture-hero of this period in its kinship history was a man called E-rets, whose name means literally "he who speaks", which might be translated as "The Word", or *logos* as the spear-point of psychic consciousness, which in later periods is so often symbolised as a two-edged sword.

The two-edged sword is such a central symbol as we have been speaking of, phallically piercing, and fashioned to strike in two directions, dividing the opposites from their incest-embrace so that they can relate more objectively.

In the Atchin village in which I lived, which was that nearest to the Malekulan mainland and thus was the most convenient centre from which the newcomers could introduce their new ideas, this culture-hero is said to have been the one who gave the final *coup de grâce* to the "closed" system of sister-exchange marriage.

In such a closed system there is no "third thing" to pierce or to disrupt the never-changing social round based on continuous repetitions of sister-exchange.

The myth told of this culture-hero is of the greatest importance for the understanding of how the human psyche works in freeing itself from an impasse such as this which has become too irksome, and of the consequent new psychic birth releasing the spirit that has been imprisoned in a social system that has given but little scope to it. The spirit in a man functions as a kind of *alter ego* which is hermaphrodite. It is thus notable that the archetypal figure of this man E-rets, whose name means "The Word" or the *logos,* is said to have had a sister who had the same name as he had himself, but with the feminine prefix *Le-*. His name was *E-rets*. Hers was *Le-rets*. His name thus indicates *logos* in its *male* aspect. Hers indicates it in its *female* aspect. Together they thus form a duality, which is the Word male-female or hermaphrodite, the *logos* in its entirety. The "third thing" was E-rets's own alleged personality combining together both opposite aspects of perception, the male and female welded into one.

The myth regarding him is told in terms of an incestuous love romance between this man and his sister, whom we will recognise as his sister-anima, since no such couple would have been allowed to live had this been a true story about human beings as they exist today.

It relates how E-rets belonged to the Atchin village of Ruruar, in which I later lived, and how his sister Le-rets had been married by her father to a husband on the Malekulan mainland, when E-rets, her brother, fell in love with her. He may have always been in love, but with their separation the passion now became acute. So he arranged with her, before she left, that if ever she heard a cock crowing in the sky above her head, she should abandon everything and come to him.

One day he made a kite. Kites are said to have been constructed in former times in Malekula by tying a woven mat to a framework of light reeds. I never saw it done, but only heard of it in this mythological setting. E-rets made such a kite, but it was of mythical proportions, for it was large enough for him to tie a cock to it. Having done this, he waited for a suitable wind, and then floated it on a dream-long string right over the half-mile wide sea-channel separating Atchin from the Malekulan mainland where his sister was at that moment sweeping out the forecourt of her husband's hut, he having gone to spend the day cultivating his garden-clearing in the bush.

The cock crew, and she looked up, and saw the cock. She left her work and, through devious bush paths, ran down to the small inlet in the coast where she knew that her brother would be, along with other Atchin folk who daily paddle their canoes over to the mainland to tend their gardens there. Once arrived near the beach, she hid herself among the trees bordering the cove till she could attract his attention by breaking twigs in the way that lovers do with pre-arranged signals. He told her to climb a tree so as not to be seen, and to wait there till dark, saying that he would be the last to come down to the shore again late in the afternoon, when his companions would already have left in their canoes to paddle back to Atchin.

He did so, and they waited there till dark, when, under cover of the night, he paddled her over to his village on Atchin and hid her with him in his hut. When morning came she was still there with him, and they stayed hidden while the others all went over to the mainland again to do their gardening. But the concealment could not last, and after a time they were of course discovered. Their father immediately threatened to drive them out, and there was an uproar in the village, his brothers joining their father in the general anathema, and they were both forced to flee.

In the myth dealing with their flight, E-rets alone is mentioned, since it is on his deed, not hers, that the myth concentrates. His hut was at the end of the village farthest from the sea, so that in fleeing he had to go through it. The myth relates however that as he fled through the village he was accosted by a man, a stranger, who befriended him, saying that he might take refuge in his hut and that he would try to placate the father and the brothers who were so outraged.

Malekulans are greedy for pigs, which are the sacrificial animals and also currency for trade, and, since this episode, have become bride-price for wives. The man proposed to pay the father in pigs, to be distributed between him and his sons, to quell their anger and as compensation for the violation of his daughter who was their sister, and at the same time to sacrifice a boar in order to placate the ancestors. The father and the brothers accepted this. The couple were allowed to stay.

The "two laws". E-rets "doubled" in personality and his whole village doubled in size
The sister-spouse in the Song of Solomon
Krishna, Portia "another Daniel"
Nebuchadnezzar and Job

If this were an ordinary story, and not a myth dealing on two levels with social change based on a *hieros gamos* with the anima, either the man and his sister would have been killed, or else she would have been sent back to her husband who would have beaten her, while E-rets himself would have had to eat very humble pie. Nor would there have been any *deus ex machina* in the form of the "friend" who seems not to have been a relative, though how he came to be there we are not told. The friend symbolises in this case an *alter ego* appearing from nowhere to support E-rets's individuality.

Nothing could demonstrate more clearly than this mythical romance that there are "two laws", that of society or collective consciousness, and that of psychic consciousness, which is its contrary. These two are complementary opposites, one based on the enforcement of the incest taboo, the other glorifying incest which, paradoxically unless we understand the flow of opposites, in fact established E-rets as the founder of the new form of social order which, far from countenancing incest, increased the scope of the incest taboo so as to make actual incest even more difficult.

For it was not only E-rets's personal development that is here mythically described. The episode describes a whole social revolution that was then taking place. It was a psychic transformation too. As in the Song of Solomon with his sister-spouse, or in the loves of Krishna[7] described in the *Bhagavad Gītā*, this psychic transformation is told in terms of the most profligate incest love. These myths, belonging to a more sophisticated age, deal only with its inner aspect. But in the case of E-rets, the union with his sister-anima gave him the strength or *mana*, not only to

---

[7] W. G. ARCHER, *The Loves of Krishna*, London, Allen and Unwin, 1957.

expand his own personality and thus get his way, but also to expand society.

Each village had at that time as its socio-religious focus one dancing-ground. E-rets now promptly founded a new dancing-ground, which meant that he was now founding a patrilineage, as over against the old sister-exchanging system which had no patrilineages.

This split the village into two, since its effect was to cause a second patrilineage to arise centering around the older dancing-ground. The village now had two patrilineages instead of none. But the two patrilineages were no longer sex rivals as in the old system of near-incestuous brothers-in-law with all the hidden jealousies and overt rules of mutual avoidance which such a system unavoidably entailed. They could be open friends. As an overt expression of this new-won patrilineal solidarity, E-rets made his new dancing-ground not separated from but actually joining the old one so that, both being in the shape of elongated ovals, the two dancing-grounds, thus joined, would, to the observer not knowing how they had arisen, appear as one very long dancing-ground which still exists.

The splitting thus had the effect, not of dividing, but of "doubling" the village, not only in the size of its dancing-ground but of its population too, each male member now having two brothers-in-law instead of one, and thus enlarging his family connections in a united double village no longer bedevilled by internal jealousies, but being now a single exogamous unit formed of two patrilineages working in basic harmony.

This led in turn to a doubling of all five patri-villages on Atchin, so that there are now in all ten patrilineages.

This semi-historical myth, one of those told on Atchin from mouth to mouth when lovers meet, or when the old instruct the young in the traditions of the tribe, has the real fairy-tale and individuation quality of the sudden, unexpected solution of a knotty problem.

It may, incidentally, throw light on other mythological cases of sister-incest on the part of gods or culture-heroes who are invariably the upholders of a moral code which forbids precisely what they are themselves said to have done. We can explain this only on lines of psychic consciousness. We may remember Shakespeare's phrase in *The Merchant of Venice* regarding Portia, that she was "another Daniel come to judgment". The Daniel of the Nebuchadnezzar story was a personification of psychic consciousness, and so was Portia who, by her Athene-like wisdom, suddenly changed everything. She was a positive anima-figure symbolised by a woman with a man's mind, propounding a law that overthrew the law, since she was psychically hermaphrodite, and thus had subtle wisdom that the others had not.

The case of E-rets and Le-rets is similar, Le-rets evoking E-rets's "other" psychic consciousness, the contrary of socially conditioned consciousness, so that he was himself in touch with both, a man so closely allied to his anima that he could challenge the world, and at the same time improve it, and be approved by it. For Le-rets was no sister in the ordinary sense of the word. She was his anima, replacing the sister or the near-incest wife of sister-exchange marriage, so that he could himself be free to marry less incestuously, not bound by the old system of sister-exchange with its closed dichotomy, but in his own person creating and founding a wider social group, thereby freeing not only himself but also society from society's own compulsion to make him marry a woman whom he did not choose.

Thus, as in the case of Nebuchadnezzar and of Job, the destruction of the former good which had become restrictive resulted not at all in disaster, but in "doubling', outwardly as well as inwardly, since E-rets thereby acquired not only a sister-anima enabling him to break through the formerly closed kinship system on his own account, but at the same time to "double" his own village of Ruruar both in its social organisation and in its size, it being now the largest and most influential village on the island.

IV.

CONCLUSIONS

The Clay and the Stone. Weakness and strength of Love

This brings us back once more to the contrast in Nebuchadnezzar's dream, the single image of the "gold" for the head symbolising the ego and the dual image of "iron and miry clay" for the feet, mentioned in the Book of Daniel. The feet are opposite in every way to the head. They are that which carry the whole body with the head on top of it, as the social system based on marriage carries the individual. The feet may here be taken as corresponding to the married state between two groups or partners which in primitive society is more rigidly a social contract than it is with us, since the elements of personal choice hardly enters in and the wife's brother (representing all her male relatives) is as important as the wife, since it is with him and with his group rather than with the individual woman that the contract is made.

Clay clearly symbolises the "soft" fleshly part of this contract, namely the personal relation between the man and the woman. Iron symbolises the "hard" part, the relationship between the men, who are the brothers-in-law.

It is iron that, in Nebuchadnezzar's image, relates to the whole body which we have taken to symbolise society, being one of the four metals of which it is composed. The clay is added as a quite different kind of substance, being wet and mouldable, the carrier of the softer emotions of individual love in at least embryonic state.

It is on account of the mouldability or "weakness" of the clay that the "stone cut out without hands" is able to shatter the otherwise impregnable image all made of metal so as to be strong and resistant to change. It was through the success of embryonic love or individual desire refusing to be regulated by parental or too great social control that the closed sister-exchanging kinship system was pierced and disrupted. The single brother-in-law who was at the same time wife's brother and sister's husband becoming changed into two, the wife's brother and the now separated sister's husband. The one relationship was "hard", that with the sister's husband with all the incest taboos surrounding it. The other, with the wife's husband, was "soft", partaking of the embryonic personal love that ego was now developing towards the wife.

These are symbolic, in Nebuchadnezzar's case, of the iron and clay which "mingle themselves with the seed of men" but "shall not cleave to one another, even as iron is not mixed with clay".

Clay symbolises weakness, the weak spot through which the otherwise rigid image became vulnerable. For weakness may sometimes have its uses. Here connected with the soft element of love, it is backed up also by the strength of the stone "cut out without hands" symbolising the corresponding strength of love or psychic consciousness, which "smote the image upon his feet that were of iron and clay, and brake them to pieces". It was the introduction of a freer choice in love in two senses, instinctive desire backed up by psychic strength, that broke the rigid system, giving rise to enlarged horizons, both social and individual.

The symbolism of the stone breaking the image of Nebuchadnezzar's identification with society as the all-embracing Male-Mother through its one soft constituent, the clay, may well be compared to the psychically matriarchal dominance of the closed sister-exchanging system yielding to the revolution that occurred in Atchin socially when the element of masculine love began to enter in, together with the notion of patrilineal descent, resulting in the five-fold system of patrilineages.

Stone and the initiating Great Mother with Ten "Sons"
The God of Light marries their Sister, thus giving rise to a collective Sister-Anima
A hundred tusked boars given in exchange

Stone has in Malekula a similar significance, for there stands a stone in the form of a natural coral monolith on the Malekulan shore, wielding the power of life or death over the dead man's ghost or spirit as, after the funeral rites, it wanders down the coast seeking the Land of the Dead on the volcano, the reaching of which confers immortality which is equivalent to psychic consciousness and "second sight", since the spirits of the ancestors symbolically living there know all that goes on in this world, so far as their descendents are concerned both in their acts and in their hearts.

This coral monolith has life, for it is one of the dwelling places of the initiating Great Mother, who devours the spirits of those who have neglected the sacrifices which she imposes, but lets those past who have not thus wasted their opportunity. It is equivalent to the moon which is a "stone", and shines like the moon at night when it lights up the grey-white coral against the background of dark bush. Both symbolise in Malekulan mythology the hardness of the incest taboo, and simultaneously its reward in psychic consciousness.

Thus, just as in life E-rets creatively made love to Le-rets his sister-anima internally, so also in the mythology the whole tribe believes in the existence of the Female Ghost or goddess who will devour if disobeyed but, if understood in her dual capacity of devourer and life-giver, will confer psychic consciousness and with it deathlessness. If a man has not properly and continuously sacrificed, she will destroy him by breaking him, one minor image for this being the breaking and thus flattening of that phallic symbol of psychic consciousness, his nose!

Just as in life Le-rets was married to her brother-animus E-rets, so also was this terrifying female goddess married in the form of her own "daughter" to the God of Light, the psychic Creator.

Not only was the Devouring Mother herself symbolised by stone, indicating that hardness which can break and divide, and also the unbreakability of the spirit arising out of her stoniness as the symbol of the incest taboo. But she engendered parthenogenically from herself ten "sons", which we may think of as corresponding to the ten *Sefiroth* or emanations of the divinity in Kabbalistic theology.

These "sons" are like their mother in being also thought of as "stones", which are to be seen standing on the coast of Atchin as ten natural coral blocks called by their name "The Ten Brothers" or "sons" of this transforming or initiating male-female principle.

It is significant that in the mythology the "god of light" was not the first thing to appear. The first was the Great Mother, the mother of all things, who, in a yet earlier form before she became stone, lived in a cave as a devouring goddess, symbolising incest itself, ready to annihilate any whom she could "eat". It was her "daughter", that is her "other" second self, that yielded to the god of light symbolising non-incest and married him. The Malekulan myth is in this respect not unlike that of the Greek Demeter, the "Earth Mother", and her daughter Persephone whom Pluto ravished by dragging her underground but did not make love to, that is to say transferred what had been outward and of the flesh into what had now become inward as the goddess of willing "death" meaning sacrifice and consequent immortality.

Although the Malekulan Great Mother turned into a stone and her ten "sons" were also stones, her daughter married by the god of light was not a stone, and is thought of as a human being. Having no father, since she was parthenogenically conceived, the daughter's guardians were (as would be the case in real life if the father were dead) her ten brothers, to whom the god of light is said to have paid for her as brideprice the quite enormous price of one hundred tusked boars for thus depriving them of their sister.

This was, according to the myth, the first time that the tusked boar as bride-price and as the sacrificial animal was introduced into Malekulan culture, meaning, from the point of view of Malekulans, to mankind in general. It was a psychically creative exchange based on the concept of the number ten (two fives), since the number of a hundred boars was made up by giving ten to each of the ten brothers, as living vessels through the rearing and sacrifice of which incest could be transformed. This was equivalent to "light", the light that pierced the "darkness" of the near-incest of sister-exchange marriage by means of the introduction of the "third element" of incest-sacrifice.

The numbers ten and one hundred have their sociological counterpart in that, owing to the doubling of the village of Ruruar through E-rets's act of incorporating his sister-anima, together with the doubling of the numbers of brothers-in-law, this village had developed two patrilineages instead of one. This had a comparable effect on all the four other Atchin villages owing to the marriages contracted with them, so that each of the five villages now had two patrilineages, and the basic number of five patrilineages was increased to ten.

Since each of these ten patrilineages regarded itself as a mirror of the whole, each patrilineage divided itself yet further for ritual purposes into ten sub-patrilineages, each with its own sub-patrilineage lodge and family name taken from that lodge. This made a hundred sub-lineages on the island of Atchin that had to be maintained, sometimes fictiously, for the proper performance of the rites. The hundred boars given for the "sister" in the myth thus corresponded with the hundred sub-lineages, all formed from the abandonment of sister-exchange marriage and thus exogamous, no member of any given lineage marrying a woman belonging to it.

The "inner light" transforms incest
Stone and the spirits of the ancestors

These all arose, according to the myth, from the single fact, which was a psychic one, of E-rets as archetypal or ideal human being acquiring a sister-anima in place of the former exchange of sisters in the flesh. Since this myth was a collective one, told throughout the island and thus having its echo in each individual psyche, there became constellated, in the mythology, the image of but one "sister-anima" for the entire island community symbolising the overcoming of sister-incest desire, which the god of light had creatively removed from men by himself marrying the "sister" of the ten mythical brothers symbolising the whole tribe. The god thus symbolises *"inner* light", that which brings consciousness through sacrifice, or letting past desires drop off which once were creative but are no longer so, in other words what we call psychic consciousness which is the sphere in which *hieros gamos* with the sister *can* take place. For this sister, the "only sister" of the ten brothers symbolising the whole tribe, now became the god's "only wife" which, in a polygamous society like the Malekulan one, means not "wife" but "anima".

This marriage with the sister-anima took place in two spheres, meaning two psychic levels, that of the god, which was repeated in more incarnated form in the myth of the "culture-hero" E-rets, thought to have been a man and actual ancestor, which functioned as a human pledge of non-incest, of which the stone monuments housing the spirits of the ancestors and the living boars sacrificed at them were the two visible symbols.

Stone, boar and "light" thus form a psychic trinity, with "light" as the dynamic factor separating the indestructible spirit from the pull of untransformed nature, the incorruptible from the corruptible, in the form of relieving the ten mythical stone-brothers from the burden of incest-desire. This gave their human counterparts, the men forming the ten patrilineages on Atchin, in recompense, a collective sister-anima symbolising that psychic function in men which in the individual mediates psychic consciousness and at the same time builds up an enlarged society.

As for the symbolism of stone, it will be remembered how stone and moon are mythologically connected. The moon, thought in Atchin to be a stone, is lit up only at night (symbolising the psychic sphere) by the god of light, who is not himself the sun but uses the sun as agent for his light. Being in her own nature cold, he warms and impregnates her with his heat and light so that she gives birth to what are called "children", but turn out on enquiry to be souls, joined to the real human children while yet in the womb, from which the children issue in due time as new-born members of the tribe.

The moon's light is *reflected light,* as the stone's light also is reflected during the daytime from the sun, and at night doubly is reflected from the moon. The white-grey stones which are the coral blocks, the only "stone" that the inhabitants of Atchin know, reflect and do not lose that light, as the surrounding bush "devours" the light by not reflecting it. For this reason among others, stones are themselves thought to have *mana* or personality, as coral blocks are held to have by reason of that reflected light, which Malekulans think of as a manifestation of spirit in general, either of mythological beings or of ancestors, depending on whether the stones are moved, or manipulated or not by man. The spirits inhabiting those not thus handled by man are thought of mainly as mythological, while those set up by man as stone monuments are thought of as housing the spirits of the ancestors, which is another way of saying the spirit of man which has been able to "move" them and thus invest them with psychic life.

It is important to realise therefore that while stone, like all matter, is of itself "female", when it is erected as a monolith it becomes "male" through the infusion into it of the transformed spirit of man which it thus inwardly reflects. "Male" symbolises that which is "set apart", as masculinity is set apart or separated from the matrix of femaleness biologically, and as the monoliths are set up and separated from the places where they are found.

The boar, on the other hand, does not reflect the light, for it is black, thus symbolising unconsciousness which is incestuous with all the unawareness of self-characterising incest in primitive mentality. For this reason the boar when untamed is regarded as the great enemy, and must be tamed, domesticated, consecrated and then sacrificed for the sake of its one imperishable object, its tusk, which shines and is crescent-shaped like the moon and symbolises the light in the darkness, or maleness in femaleness, and is, for the Malekulan who has sacrificed his boar and thus obtained its tusk, the symbol for his own personal *mana* or psychic consciousness.

The boars destined for sacrifice are brought out from the places where they have been reared and tied to the monoliths containing the spirits of the ancestors so that the spirits may witness the sacrifice. For each successive rite there are erected ten such monoliths, symbolising the ten patrilineages and the mythical Ten Stone Brothers. Each monolith has further nine small upright stones set alongside it, so that there are a hundred stones in all, each stone having its sacrificial boar tied to it, corresponding to the myth in which the god of light had given ten boars to each of the ten brothers as bride-price for their one common sister.

The ancestors thus now symbolically witnessing the sacrifice were once human beings who had themselves similarly sacrificed and thus created their own spirits, so that the monuments set up commemorating them are reminders of the psychic work they did upon themselves. These stones in turn yet further symbolise the spirits of the living men who erect them, who are the descendants of those ten lines of ancestors whose spirits inform the stones, and whose public and inner sacrifices their descendants repeat.

Collectively, these hewn stones may be thought of as one, symbolising the whole tribal spirit, which continues to be "made" with each successive sacrifice, as the stones are cut out from their matrix and "made" into monoliths, symbolising the firmness and durability of the spirit they represent. Symbolic of spirit, they may be compared therefore to the stone "cut out without hands" of Nebuchadnezzar's dream, which "smote the earth" and "became a great mountain, and filled the whole earth".

In point of fact, symbolically, the Malekulan stone does "fill the whole earth", since there is no man, woman or child for instance on Atchin who does not belong to one of the ten lineages thus symbolised by hewn stone, humanly corresponding to the ten natural coral blocks symbolising the ten mythical brothers, all said to have been "born" out of the one tall monolithic stone symbolising the Great Mother in her phallic aspect as the Initiatress into the world of men and thus the psychic world.

Destruction precedes rebirth
The withholding soul yields her treasure up

The motive of destruction preceding rebirth is to be seen not only in general terms in the destruction of the old near-incest sister-exchanging system, so that a broader and less restrictive social system might arise out of it and the spirit of man progressively be freed. It is seen in particular at each repeated sacrifice when, witnessed by the ancestors present in the stone monuments, the boar symbolising incest is slain and out of it flows into the sacrificer the spirit of this same incest transformed into that *mana* or psychic substance, or psychic consciousness, the acquirement of which is the object of the sacrifice.

This power comes ultimately from the marriage of the god of light with the dark power of the earth goddess in the form of her daughter whose brothers were willing to give their sister up in exchange for a sister-anima.

So also the withholding soul may yield up her treasure if ego can but sacrifice enough its own incestuous self-identification, and dare to put its trust in its more knowledgable contrasexuality, however illegitimate or mad this may at first appear, as did E-rets's union with his "sister-wife", for the sake of doubling himself and so becoming whole, male and female in one, like the Malekulan who becomes the "Lord Mother", including mother of himself.

Daniel's interpretation of Nebuchadnezzar's dreams and the result which followed in Nebuchadnezzar's case, backed up by the book of Job, concur with the Malekulan evidence that, once this is accomplished, society itself will bend, since deprivation rightly understood and truly accepted will open the way to a new access of psychic consciousness, which in the end doubles the personality by giving back all that had been sacrificed, in a form that can no more be lost.

List of Author's Works referred to in the text

From "Eranos-Jahrbuch":

1937, Vol. V   *Der Mythos der Totenfahrt auf Malekula*
1945, Vol. XII *The Incest Taboo and the Virgin Archetype*
1948, Vol. XVI *The Making of Man in Malekula*
1955, Vol. XXIV *Identification with the Sacrificial Animal*

Other sources:

1942, *Stone Men of Malekula*, London, Chatto and Windus.
1955, *Boar-Sacrifice*, "Journal of Analytical Psychology", Vol. I, No. 1.
1958, *The Four-hundred year old Dream of a Pacific Islander*, in: *"Geist und Werk, Aus der Werkstatt unserer Autoren"*, Rhein-Verlag, Zurich 1959.
1959, *Homo-eroticism in Primitive Society as a Function of the Self,* paper read at the First International Congress for Analytical Psychology, held in Zurich in August 1958, published in "The Journal of Analytical Psychology", Vol. 4, No. 2.

Works by other authors referred to where mentioned in the text.

BIBLIOGRAPHY OF JOHN LAYARD'S WRITINGS

1. Catalogue of the Layard Collection in the Cambridge Museum of Archaeology and of Ethnology, no date.

2. "Degree-Taking Rites in South-West Bay, Malekula", *Journal of the Royal Anthropological Institute*, 58, London, 1928.

3. "Malekula: Flying Tricksters, Ghosts, Gods and Epileptics", *Journal of the Royal Anthropological Institute*, 60, London, 1930.

4. "The Journey of the Dead from the Small Islands of North-Eastern Malekula", in *Essays Presented to C. G. Seligman*, London, 1934.

5. "Atchin Twenty Years Ago", *Geographical Journal*, 88, London, 1936.

6. "Maze Dances and the Ritual of the Labyrinth in Malekula", *Folk-Lore*, 47, London, 1936.

7. "Labyrinth Ritual in South India: Threshold and Taboo Designs", *Folk-Lore*, 48, London, 1937.

8. "Der Mythos der Totenfahrt auf Malekula", *Eranos-Jahrbuch*, 5, Zürich (Rhein-Verlag), 1937. Revised and expanded version translated by Ralph Manheim in *Spiritual Disciplines: Papers from the Eranos Yearbooks*, 4, entitled "The Malekulan Journey of the Dead", London (Routledge) and New York (Pantheon), 1960.

9. *Stone Men of Malekula*, London (Chatto and Windus), 1942.

10. "Incarnation and Instinct", *Guild of Pastoral Psychology*, Lecture 27, London, 1944.

11. "Primitive Kinship as Mirrored in the Psychological Structure of Modern Man", *British Journal of Medical Psychology*, 20, London, 1944.

12. *The Lady of the Hare*, London (Faber and Faber), 1944.

13. "The Incest Taboo and the Virgin Archetype", *Eranos-Jahrbuch*, 12, Zürich (Rhein-Verlag), 1945.

14. "The Making of Man in Malekula", *Eranos-Jahrbuch*, 16, Zürich (Rhein-Verlag), 1949.

15. "The Pilgrimage to Oba: an Atchin Sex-Initiation Rite", *South-Sea Studies*, Basel, (Museum für Völkerkunde), 1951.

16. "The Role of the Sacrifice of Tusked Boars in Malekulan Religion and Social Organisation", *Actes du Congrès International des Sciences Anthropologiques et Ethnologiques*, 2, Vienna, 1952. Reprinted in *Harvest*, London, 1954.

17. "Kinship and Marriage", in E. E. Evans-Pritchard (ed.), *The Institutions of Primitive Society*, Oxford (Blackwell), 1956. German translation by Bärman in *Institutionen in primitiven Gesellschaften*, Frankfurt-am-Main (Suhrkamp), 1967.

18. "Boar Sacrifice", *Journal of Analytical Psychology*, 1/1, London, 1955.

19. "Identification with the Sacrifical Animal", *Eranos-Jahrbuch*, 24, Zürich (Rhein-Verlag), 1956.

20. "The Four-Hundred-Year-old Kinship Dream of a Pacific Islander", in *Geist und Werk*, Zürich (Rhein-Verlag), 1958.

21. "Note on the Autonomous Psyche and the Ambivalence of the Trickster Concept", *Journal of Analytical Psychology*, 3/1, London, 1958.

22. "Homo-eroticism in Primitive Society as a Function of the Self", *Journal of Analytical Psychology*, 4/2, London, 1959. Reprinted in Gerhard Adler(ed.), *Current Trends in Analytical Psychology*, London (Tavistock), 1961.

23. "On Psychic Consciousness", *Eranos-Jahrbuch*, 28, Zürich (Rhein-Verlag), 1960.

24. "The Meaning of Medicine", *British Homeopathic Journal*, 1/2, April, 1961.

UNPUBLISHED PAPERS

25. *Changes in the Kinship Systems of the Small Islands of Malekula* (800 pp. ms. approx.)

26. *Myth, Religion and Ritual on the Malekulan Small Island of Atchin* (800 pp. ms. approx.)

27. "Primitive Kinship for the Psychologist".

28. *The Snake, the Dragon and the Tree:* a case-history illustrated by the patient's paintings (The Mary Book).

29. *The Fisherman's Daughter:* a case-history.

30. "Psychosomatic Opposites: a case of psoriasis and cancer".

31. *The Welsh Myth Cullwch and Olwen from the Mabinogion.*

R. J. Woolger